SCUDAMORE
ON
STEEPLECHASING

Also by Peter Scudamore with Alan Lee
A Share of Success

SCUDAMORE
ON
STEEPLECHASING

by Peter Scudamore with Alan Lee

PARTRIDGE PRESS

LONDON · NEW YORK · TORONTO · SYDNEY · AUCKLAND

TRANSWORLD PUBLISHERS LTD
61–63 Uxbridge Road, London W5 5SA

TRANSWORLD PUBLISHERS (AUSTRALIA) PTY LTD
15–23 Helles Avenue, Moorebank, NSW 2170

TRANSWORLD PUBLISHERS (NZ) LTD
Cnr Moselle and Waipareira Aves,
Henderson, Auckland

Published 1988 by Partridge Press
a division of Transworld Publishers Ltd
Copyright © Peter Scudamore and Alan Lee 1988

Designed by Graeme Murdoch

British Library Cataloguing in Publication Data

Scudamore, Peter
Scudamore on steeplechasing.
1. Great Britain. Steeplechasing
I. Title II. Lee, Alan, 1954–
798.4'5'0941

ISBN 1-85225-041-0

Printed in West Germany by
Mohndruck Graphische Betriebe Gmbh, Gütersloh

CONTENTS

1
THE ROUTINE

THE MOST CERTAIN aspect of a jump jockey's existence is that nothing is certain. Each day begins with a series of imponderables and ends, invariably, with a sequence of surprises upon which to reflect. Little is ever what it seems. Nothing can be taken for granted. It would not do for some – those who crave an ordered life of consistent routine and predictable hours would hate it – but then, I guess, anyone of such regulated tastes would never even contemplate entering this crazy old world in which I live.

It would be quite wrong, however, to give the impression that jockeys live in a cocoon of chaos. We may never be sure what the next week, the next day or even the next ride will bring, but there is a large amount of planning essential to the job. There is also, inevitably, a certain routine to the make-up of each week, as well as the punctuation of delights, frustrations and occasional agonies which can never be accurately predicted by either the best or the worst among us.

To give an initial idea of a jockey's life, let's look at Sundays. The one day of the week when there is no racing (although even that may not be the case for too many more years), Sunday is still not entirely a day of rest. For trainers, of course, it is much like any other day in the yard – the horses still have to be fed and exercised; for jockeys, it is chiefly a day on which the coming week is mapped out.

Sunday is the one morning on which a jockey is not especially anxious to be up with the lark. However, there are times when it is necessary. If one of my regular trainers asks me to come and school a couple of young horses on a Sunday morning, then of course I will be there. In my case, this can mean a very early start and a disruption of the entire day. It would be a chore if the journey were to school a horse of doubtful ability which I might never ride anyway, but if I can see a successful end product, I soon forget that it is supposed to be a day of leisure.

My ideal Sunday during the racing season pans out something like this. I wake later than usual, although with two young sons a lie-in is never likely to extend much beyond breakfast time. Most of the morning is then spent on the telephone; in this regard, it is the busiest time of the week. As a matter of routine, I ring Fred Winter's assistant Charlie Brooks (who has now taken over the licence since Mr Winter's accident last year), Martin Pipe and Nick Gaselee. These, in that order, are my three main stables and other than in exceptional circumstances I will always make myself available for their runners first. Once I have a clear idea of their intentions, I will be pretty sure at which meeting I will be riding on each day of the coming week. I can then concentrate on the remaining races – those in which none of my three yards has a runner – and investigate the chances of picking up a decent spare ride.

There was a time when I would ride anything that was offered and would go out of my way even to get on horses of highly dubious ability. I can't afford to be so cavalier now; with so many good horses to ride, I need to be discerning about my spares. I am first of all looking for something with a chance of winning, secondly something with a future and thirdly – but not least important – something which is not odds-on to land me in hospital. Sometimes, of course, it is the safest and speediest of mounts that give you the worst falls, and there is no way of avoiding your share, but equally there is nothing to be gained and much to be lost by taking a chance on horses whose jumping is at best suspect.

Shortly before lunch, the phone will be put down with an air of finality. The next few hours are precious, private hours with the family – heaven knows, there is little enough time during the season – and like most other racing folk of my acquaintance, I resent the phone ringing on a Sunday afternoon. In fact, I probably won't answer it! This is the only time in the week which I can devote to home affairs without regular interruptions, and it would be very unfair to all if I compromised it. Nevertheless there are times, especially in the summer, when I am asked to present prizes at open days or to attend garden fetes, and I accept whenever possible because these are events for all the family.

Food and drink rationing is relaxed on a Sunday. On Saturday evenings, driving home after a day's racing, Monday always seems a long way off. There is a dangerous temptation to be carried away by the sense of freedom, but a few drinks too many on a Saturday night inevitably brings a remorseful, abstemious Sunday, so I prefer to have a relatively quiet Saturday – sometimes a meal out with friends, often never venturing out at all – and then indulge myself with a proper British Sunday lunch. I will always be a pound or two heavier on Mondays than on any other racing day.

Whenever possible, I go to church on Sunday evening. Then, providing I don't have to be too light the following day, I might have another snack meal. I will be in bed by nine and asleep soon afterwards. It may seem startlingly early to some, but almost every Monday morning I have to be up and about by 5.30 a.m. – and that does not sit comfortably with a late night, as I know to my cost. Braving the pre-dawn hours on a freezing, unfriendly winter morning is seldom a pleasure, even after a quiet, sober evening and a full eight hours' sleep. It can make me feel positively ill if I have stayed up too late, eating and drinking too freely. Not every jockey finds it necessary to live frugally or to take such determined care over sleeping hours; there are those who happily get by with much less sleep and regularly dine and drink late. But I know it would not work for me, and as long as I am a professional jockey I intend to maintain a professional outlook, even if it does mean a degree of self-denial.

I usually reap the benefit of this approach when the alarm clock wakes me on Monday mornings. It would be foolish to pretend that I leap out of bed with an entirely light heart. After all, the time is just before 5.30 a.m. and it is the first day of the working week. Jockeys are not vastly different from the rest of the population in a dread of Monday mornings; in our case it is not just the start of another week but the day on which racing is generally at its most mundane, in terms of both quality and venues. It is very much a case of 'another day at the office', without any appetising highlights. However, for me and many other jockeys there is much to be done even before we arrive at the races. Providing the day's meeting is not too far north, I habitually spend both Monday and Tuesday mornings schooling for my Lambourn trainers. Fred Winter's horses pull out of

Uplands at 7.45 a.m.; Nick Gaselee's string is in action fifteen minutes earlier. I always aim to be in Lambourn a quarter of an hour before the horses pull out, which means setting off from my Cotswolds home no later than 6 a.m.

Shift workers, milkmen and postmen will appreciate the problems of creeping around in the dark at an ungodly hour, trying hard not to rouse the rest of the family. I never see my two sons before I leave the house in the mornings and, naturally, my wife Marilyn is not keen to have them woken and then abandoned to her! I give breakfast a miss – not even bothering with the cup of tea or coffee without which so many people apparently find it impossible to get moving in the morning. I collect *The Sporting Life* from the local newsagents, where I am regularly the first customer, and then head south towards Berkshire accompanied only by my car stereo.

We jockeys clock up a great many miles in the course of a season, and, although I quite enjoy driving I sometimes think I would go mad without my music to help pass the time. I suppose I have rather extraordinary tastes. Bruce Springsteen, Dire Straits and the Eurythmics are belted out on my system most days, but I also delve into the more obscure areas of rock and pop music. Classics I leave alone; I think they would tend to depress me while battling back along the M25 after a fraught day on the slopes at Plumpton.

Once in Lambourn, there is no time for niceties. A few curt 'good mornings' and then we are off to the Downs for that part of a jockey's life which is very much more private and less glamorous than the public front at the races, although in many cases it is just as important. I am a big believer in the 'practice makes perfect' adage, and it appals me to see some young horses dispatched for their hurdling or chasing débuts quite patently without the first idea of what is expected of them. It is certainly true that some horses need and benefit from schooling more than others, but in my view it is unforgivable to ignore the education process completely.

Having a lot of horses to ride has changed my attitude towards schooling. I am now much more realistic about what a horse can do. Some trainers, especially those who are struggling along with only a few horses, are so determined to see the best in them, so dangerously close to them in fact, that they might be delighted by a schooling performance which was in reality no better than mildly encouraging. It can sometimes be difficult to bring a habitual optimist down to earth, but I strongly believe it is for everyone's good to know the truth about a horse's progress and, sometimes, to accept that there is a good bit more work to be done before launching him on to a racecourse.

Martin Pipe asked me recently why, when schooling a horse over fences for the first time, I will leave him alone to fiddle the first obstacle rather than ask him for a long one to show his capabilities. My answer is that schooling should be simulating race conditions as closely as possible – I would never fire a young horse into the first fence in a novice chase, so why do it on the schooling grounds and take the risk of a bad mistake, or even a fall, which might set the horse's confidence back a long way? To get a horse on the floor at home simply through trying to go too fast or jump too boldly is foolish; it undoes all the good that the schooling may have achieved.

My value as a schooling jockey, and the value of any rider worth his salt, lies in the ability to advise a trainer. If a horse starts mulishly kicking his hurdles out of the ground, or has simply lost confidence in his jumping, I might suggest that he be sent to one of the jumping specialists such as Charles Radclyffe or Henrietta Knight who, by hours of meticulous practice, will teach an ignorant or errant horse to pick up his feet. A trainer in charge of a large number of horses simply does not have time to devote such attention to an individual animal.

Many horses will react totally differently to their schooling behaviour when confronted with the hurly-burly of a racecourse. I have known horses who are brilliant jumpers on the schooling grounds go completely to pieces in a racing environment. Equally, I have seen plenty who are reluctant, sketchy jumpers at home somehow inspired and transformed when put under competitive pressure. There are, of course, just as many whose work at home gives a perfectly accurate guide to their chances in a race, but experience convinces me that the betting coups one hears so often at the planning stage ('he's a certainty – jumps like a buck at home') are in most cases believed only by the gullible and the desperate.

Schooling will be over shortly after nine o'clock. Back at the yard, I will then spend ten minutes in the office with the trainer, discussing entries and riding plans for various horses. At the beginning and end of the season I might also drink a cup of coffee, but in mid-winter there is no time. Racing starts at midday, or soon after, and as I always aim to be on the course an hour before the first race, my schedule is very tight. A word with the head lad is both polite and important, as he is the man closest to the horses, day in, day out. Then it is back in the car and on the road again.

When people question me about the tedium of driving to meetings six days a week I always answer that it is not the going which bothers me – it is the coming back. On the way to the course, there is always plenty to keep my mind occupied. The hopes and uncertainties of the day lie ahead. By the time I leave the course I will probably be tired and hungry, it will often be dark, frequently raining or worse, and another two hours or so on the road can seem a very daunting prospect. Most tracks on my usual circuit are within two and a half hours of home (Folkestone, at upwards of three, is the worst journey), but this time can obviously be greatly increased during the bad weather we are usually obliged to suffer in the worst of winter.

In many ways I enjoy the solitude of driving. It gives me time to think, to plan and to wind down. Occasionally, however, I enjoy the luxury of being chauffered, with the freedom to have a nap, use the car phone or simply read the paper. The car phone is a godsend. Trainers are always able to contact me on the road – and normally I am on the road at the time of the morning they want to ring me – and I am able to make my routine morning calls, which can sometimes take up to an hour, in warmth and comfort. As for the reading of *The Sporting Life*, this may sound like a spell of gentle relaxation but in fact it is an essential task each day. Not only must I familiarise myself with the form of the opposition in all the races I am contesting, I also have to study the advance four-day declarations for the rest of the week, sorting out possible rides and then making the relevant phone calls.

There is a distinct difference in status between the jet-setting flat jockeys and us jumping boys. Once he has attained a certain standard, it is very rare to find a flat jockey driving himself anywhere – if he goes by car at all he will usually have an agent or a friend to drive him, and quite frequently he will travel by plane or helicopter. There are no such luxuries in our game, and the most I can hope for is that my father will be free to take over the wheel on the odd day.

Once at the racecourse I feel I am very much on public display, not just in silks on the track but wherever I might go before and after the meeting. In other words, I think it is very important to look smart. I will change into racing clothes wherever and whenever the opportunity arises and, while I will invariably dress more casually for, say, Taunton or Fontwell than I would for a major meeting at Ascot or Newbury, I can't remember ever being on a racecourse in jeans, or without a tie. It is a personal thing; Steve Smith Eccles frequently wears jeans yet still manages to look smart, while John Francome would often arrive in what most people would term unconventional dress. He was good enough to get away with it – Francome could have gone racing with nothing on at all and still got a bookful of rides – but for most of us, making the right impression on influential people is part of the everyday job. I cannot understand young jockeys (and there are plenty of them) who turn up at courses looking as if they have just rolled in from a fairground. Open-necked shirts, jeans and unruly hair tend to give you a bad start in dealing with the people who hand out the good things in racing. Again, I may well have started with an advantage here, because my father was a great believer in dressing properly for racing and his views have naturally been inherited.

Ideally I would like to go straight into a sauna when I arrive at the racecourse. In practical terms this is usually impossible because so few racetracks provide this basic facility. At Sandown and Cheltenham, where the saunas are excellent, it is part of my regular routine to spend up to an hour in there before racing; at most other places the saunas are either inadequate or non-existent, and this rates as one of my most consistent general complaints. I cannot make ten stone without a sauna, and although I have a perfectly good one at home, there is no time to use it on winter mornings when I have to go out and school. There are jockeys who claim that it is possible to lose seven pounds during an hour in a sauna, but I think three pounds is a more realistic target. If you are fighting to lose much more than that, you probably should not have taken the ride in the first place.

The weighing room is the jockeys' sacred territory on any racecourse. It is not exactly inviolate, as trainers tend to wander in and out quite regularly and there are occasional interlopers with less legitimate business. But it is our domain, the place where we not only prepare for rides, but let off steam afterwards. The only men privy to all this, and consequently very much our friends and trusted confidants, are the valets. There are two at most run-of-the-mill meetings, three at the major days, and very often the qualified valets will have an assistant with them. There is nothing random about their duties – each of them has certain jockeys to 'do', those jockeys probably staying with them throughout their career. My valet is John Buckingham, the former jockey best known for winning the Grand National on 100 to 1 shot Foinavon in 1967. 'Buck' looks after many of the southern jockeys. His job includes taking all our tack from meeting to meeting and setting it up in each weighing room. It also includes cleaning up the tack when we have finished with it which, on some of the boggy winter days we have to encounter, can be a pretty thankless task.

14

Almost everywhere we go, I know exactly where I will be changing. I also know, as soon as I walk into the weighing room, which of my friends are at the same meeting. There is, you see, a set pattern in the changing quarters – a pecking order, if you like. When John Francome was still riding he, naturally, was head of the weighing room and had pole position on every course. Now that privilege has passed to Steve Smith Eccles, partly on grounds of experience and partly because he moans more than the rest of us! I change in the number two slot, next to him, followed by Hywel Davies, Richard Rowe and Simon Sherwood.

It is quite a clubby environment and the youngsters – the newcomers – have to earn their promotion the hard way. This may sound suspiciously like a 'them and us' situation, and in some ways that is an apt description. It is not mere snobbery, though. Each time a new, fresh-faced lad arrives in the weighing room, we older hands have to regard him as a potential threat to us, a possible danger on the course. Jump racing is a risky business, but the risks can be minimised by sensible jockeys. I know that if I am in a novice chase with Steve, Hywel and Simon, there will be an element of co-operation. By this I do not mean a carve-up of who is going to win (things like that really do happen only in the pages of novels – it's hard enough to win a jump race without plotting to give one away) but a tacit understanding that we are not going to cut each other up by all scrapping for the inside rail on the approach to the first. There is an area of give and take within the competitive framework of any race, and the physical safety of both horse and jockey can never be entirely forgotten in a cut-throat desire to win. Young jockeys are naturally out to make their name, and most have neither the skill to keep their horses straight nor the sense to avoid riding in a way that would earn a conviction for dangerous driving on a motorway. I am quite sure that I was just the same in my early days. The secret of success is to learn the lessons quickly.

The weighing room is very much more than just a place to change clothes. It is where jockeys will build themselves up and where they will wind down again; it is where jokes will inevitably be told; and it is also where, occasionally, the internal rows and resentments that jump racing inevitably breeds will spill over into something ugly. In my time as a jockey I have only ever seen two fist fights between jockeys in the weighing room, and while that is undoubtedly two too many, it is also a surprisingly small number when the pressures of race riding at this intensely competitive level are considered. Most days at least one on-course disagreement will spill over into a full-blown argument in the weighing room. Very often, an inexperienced claimer or an incompetent rider is involved. Jockeys are always being unnecessarily cut up during races and, when the innocent party feels he has been deprived of a winner or a placing by the ignorance of another rider, tempers are bound to fray. If the row is conducted within the weighing room, away from the public eye, I don't think anyone should complain; just occasionally, however, there have been undignified cases of jockeys squabbling on the way off the course, which does nothing for the sport's image.

As in any group of fellow workers, whether they share an office, a factory floor or a racecourse weighing room, there are those who have plenty to say every day while others remain virtually silent and introspective throughout a meeting. John Francome was not only the best jockey of his time, he was also very much the central character of the weighing room, forever regaling us with his latest gag or selecting a new victim for a practical joke. Steve Smith Eccles is now possibly the noisiest of our number, but Welshman Hywel Davies, like many of his countrymen, is never happy when not speaking.

It may surprise some to know that we don't spend all our time talking racing. Light relief may come in the form of a debate on television programmes, new cars or the latest in video equipment. As with any job, it is possible to become too immersed, too blinkered, and the outside world can sometimes seem a shade remote from our regular closed circuit of stables–motorway–racecourse. Naturally, however, much of the weighing-room chat does revolve around racing, be it horses, jockeys, courses or characters. There will be a daily discussion on the identity of the clerk of the scales, the official who has the most bearing on our afternoon. Understandably, some are looked upon by jockeys with more favour than others. The starter is another official with whom we have close contact throughout the meeting; again, in our eyes, there are some very good ones and some we would rather avoid. The stewards might get a mention if there has been a contentious inquiry. Something, you may be sure, has always happened during the day to stimulate an animated debate.

For me, the weighing room is also the place for an occasional spot of self-motivation. I never found this necessary when I was younger and fresh to the job. Now, a little older, a lot wiser and perhaps a shade more cynical, I do have to stoke myself up on certain days. There are times when, quite by coincidence, I will ride a string of bad horses. When that happens the tendency is for my sights to be lowered. Winning is replaced in the forefront of my mind by survival. At times like these, a soccer player (or those in most other team sports) can expect help from his manager. A jockey has to sort himself out, and there are days when it is not easy. For some reason, my confidence is often low on a Monday. Maybe it is that it's the start of the week, maybe that the quality of horses on that day is usually modest; but whatever the reason, I feel sure that the jockey's inhibitions must transmit themselves to the horse beneath him. I have worked on this problem and tried

THE ROUTINE

Occasionally, it can be a joy to get out of bed and on horseback before the milkman has called. At certain times of year, it is no kind of pleasure. Riding out at Lambourn under the pre-dawn streetlights of winter contrasts with the summer scene at Condicote, where David Nicholson and The Princess Royal are among those accompanying me.

OFFICIAL GOING
GOOD
TRAINER STATES
3RD RACE. N.° 1
4TH RACE 14.
6TH RACE 4.5.13.18.19.
WILL NOT RUN

APPROX ODDS

There is far more to the ritual
of race days than sitting on the
horses. Jockeys spend a lot of
time studying form in the racing
papers; a lot more talking tactics
with their trainers; and the period
between races is a frantic rush to
change colours.

The snowy scene was Cheltenham Gold Cup day
1987 – thankfully, we do not often have to encounter
conditions quite so extreme. (Above right) Talking
over a winner with a suitably satisfied guv'nor, Fred
Winter. (Below right) Missing out by a nostril in a
photo-finish, that most galling of defeats.

Bolands Cross, trained at Lambourn by Nick Gaselee, is one of the most exciting 'chasers I have ridden.

Run and Skip, a great credit to his trainer John Spearing, on his way to victory in the 1986 Anthony Mildmay–Peter Cazalet Chase at Sandown.

A family triumph for a firm friend – Mrs Muck, owned and trained by Nigel Twiston-Davies, led in by her loving stablelass, Marilyn Scudamore.

to minimise its cause and effect, but it has to be faced that no jockey, however good or bad, can operate at a hundred per cent efficiency all the time, six days a week.

Next stop after the weighing room is the parade ring. First ride of the day, and I have an owner who smirks knowingly and confides: 'This one will win.' I sigh inwardly and try to remain impassive. I have heard it so often before, and such exaggerated confidence is usually the prelude to a shattering disappointment for all concerned. I take no notice now whenever an owner or a trainer says something along those lines; I have never yet ridden a sure thing and I don't suppose I am ever likely to. Those who brag that their horses are 'certainties' are invariably covering up their own insecurity and seeking a show of reassurance from the jockey. I'm afraid I no longer oblige. The most I like to hear in the way of encouragement before a race is something more modest such as: 'This one jumps well and has a really good chance.'

The majority of owners will have a punt on their horse, whether in fun, interest or serious belief. There is, however, a difference between the average man having a modest £10, £20 or even £50 on his horse and the genuine gambling owner – the man who has assessed that this will be his day and has staked a fortune, which frequently he can't afford. Every jockey will occasionally be confronted by this predicament. When it does happen, it is assuredly best to be unaware of it until the race is over. There are, of course, gamblers who cannot resist telling their jockey, while standing in the parade ring, exactly how much money they have invested in his abilities. With some this is mere bravado, with others a cover for their nerves or their underlying lack of confidence. Whatever the motive, it is of absolutely no help to the poor jockey, who has enough to worry about in trying to win the race without the pressure of knowing the extent of the fortune wagered on his success. Inevitably, if the horse is beaten and the owner left virtually broke, the rider will fear that he is somehow to blame for this plight, no matter how good a race he may have ridden.

It is much more acceptable when an owner tells his jockey that he has backed his horse each way and is very keen to finish in the frame. That knowledge can be useful: if the horse is tired and has no chance of winning, a jockey may be more inclined to give him a hard race in the hope of salvaging third place if he knows it will please the owner.

Straight after a race we meet up again with the connections, hopefully in the winners' enclosure but more often in that nomadic area, a little detached from the celebrations, where the also-rans unsaddle. It is at this point that the jockey should have something useful to say. I try never simply to tell an owner that his horse is useless. There are jockeys who have done this with brutal frankness, and while some of them have been among the most successful at their job, I am certain that it must have cost them rides. You have to remember that the great majority of jump-racing owners are in the game for fun, for the social side and for something to talk about with their friends. Many of them have utterly false impressions about the prospects of their 'pet' racehorses, but I do not consider it a jockey's duty to disillusion them; if anyone is to do that it should be the trainer. The other factor against dismissing a horse as useless is, of course, that the animal is then sure to prove you a fool the very next time he runs!

18

Owners who have been disappointed by a poor showing are invariably hoping that the jockey will offer an excuse that they can then pass on to all the friends and family who had been firmly advised that the horse would win. This, of course, can be hard. The truth is that horses are not machines; at whatever level they are competing they cannot win all the time, and the reason for a bad run may simply be that the horse was feeling off-colour. It happens to humans, after all – although try telling that to a deflated owner!

The furthest I may go in condemning a horse is to say that he is basically slow, that he is a poor jumper, or maybe that he gave me no 'feel', that term beloved by jockeys that is a mystery to people outside the game but an intangible attribute of all decent racehorses. It is for me to advise the owner and trainer how his horse should best be ridden in future engagements (whether or not I keep the ride), and to suggest what distance, type of course and standard of race to aim for. If I say that a horse 'might win a little seller at Bangor-on-Dee', that is as close as I can go to implying that the horse is no good. Some owners are horrified by such advice, but all I can say is that it is meant constructively and intended to be mutually beneficial – after all, if I am going to continue riding a particular horse, I want it to be placed in a grade where it has a chance of providing me with a winner.

The opposite danger, in these ritualistic post-mortems, is to tell an owner that he has a world-beater on his hands. Not only is this most unlikely to be the case, it is a careless statement which will probably come back to haunt the jockey who utters it. Buoyed up by the emotion of a decent win, and deluded by the back-slapping atmosphere, it is all too easy to go overboard in the horse's praise without having had the opportunity to weigh up all the factors (was he a lucky winner? what was the standard of the opposition? is his jumping likely to find him out? – and a dozen other complications). No matter how impressed I may be on jumping off a horse, I always try to keep my feet, and the owner's, on the ground. An owner will always remember what you say about his horse. The jockey will probably forget his words once he has gone through the same process with two or three other owners; but for each of those owners only one horse matters, and it is vital to remember that. Being accurate, compassionate and realistic in post-race assessments does get me rides, of that I am convinced.

There are times, inevitably, when I come back in the full knowledge that I have made a mess of things, that for some reason I have made an error in the course of the race and that, even if it has not cost the chance of victory, it has meant the horse running some way below his optimum. I have tried diligently to cut out my mistakes and I believe that each season I have eliminated a little more margin for error. But racing is all about split-second decisions; jockeys are not robots, and all of us will occasionally ride a stinker of a race. If you are worth your salt you will always know when you have done so, and you will always feel bad about it. I certainly brood when I am aware that I have ridden badly, and I dislike getting off the horse to be told what I did wrong – in my view, it is unnecessary. Days like those end for me with a mood of depression, a thoughtful journey home, a regrettable snappiness with my wife and an evening of self-recrimination. You might think that I have been riding long enough to have got beyond this by now, but I promise you that my depressions are every bit as black as when I started out. Thankfully, it only needs a winner to put me right again.

Before going home, I like to have a reflective period relaxing in the weighing room. I also like to have something to eat, usually my first food of the day. My regular diet is a sandwich or a pie, along with a cup of tea, followed by a leisurely shower. John Buckingham is always teasing me about being the last to leave the weighing room at night, but that winding-down spell is important to me. It also makes practical good sense, as I am not one of those who head straight for the bar after racing, and on most courses there is no chance of a fast escape from the car park immediately after the last race.

Back home, I will try to spend some time with my boys before dealing with the inevitable batch of phone calls, both incoming and outgoing. I have a mobile phone and now wonder how I ever managed without it – I carry it everywhere around the house and, between the hours of six and eight, I spend more time on it than not. With the business finished I will allow myself a glass or two of wine and an evening meal. I might watch television, though I am by no means an addict. Most of it I consider an utter waste of time. I hate soap operas because I think they are an inane escape from reality, but I do enjoy certain comedies – *M.A.S.H., Alas Smith and Jones, Only Fools and Horses* and *Auf Wiedersehen Pet* are among my favourites. Soon it is nine o'clock and time for bed, before the whole routine starts again some while before the dawn. □

2
THE MOUNTS

BROADSWORD: Whatever else may happen in my riding career, I shall always have a very deep affection for Broadsword. Ours was a special relationship. We helped to establish each other at the top, and although at championship level (twice in succession at the Cheltenham festival) there was intense disappointment, Broadsword won enough quality races to be judged one of the best hurdlers of his time.

There are some horses whose work at home bears no relation to performances on the racetrack, but Broadsword was instantly recognisable as a high-class horse as soon as he came into David Nicholson's yard. His flat rating indicated as much, of course, but achievements on the level have never been a guaranteed passport to success at jumping; many is the time a trainer has spent a lot of money buying a quality flat horse only to find that he has no aptitude whatever for hurdling. With Broadsword we never had any such worries. When we first took him to the races it was quickly apparent that he was more forward, more mature, than almost all of his generation.

Broadsword started his three-year-old career one autumn Saturday at Kempton Park. It was a relief rather than a surprise when he won comfortably, the first of seven victories in a season when he was plainly the top juvenile hurdler right up to the time when it mattered most, the day of the *Daily Express* Triumph Hurdle at Cheltenham. The Triumph is always one of the toughest races of the jumping calendar, not only to ride in but also to assess. There is only the one season's form to work on, and much of that may be unreliable. The best horses can often encounter problems in running because there is always a maximum field, and the race regularly turns up a surprise. This particular year was no exception.

Broadsword went off a ludicrously short-priced favourite. I say that while admitting that I could see no horse among the opposition which should logically have been capable of beating him at level weights. He had, it is true, been beaten once – at Sandown Park – but there were genuine reasons for that and we had convincingly seen off the other fancied horses in the Triumph field whenever we had come up against them.

We had no complicated plan for the race. My instructions were simply to keep Broadsword out of trouble and make sure that he was not so far off the pace that he had too much to do at the business end of the race. Essentially, he was an athletic animal, a superb jumper and a refreshingly enthusiastic galloper. But he did not have the electrifying turn of foot at the end of the race; he had to be close enough to make his stamina and his jumping tell.

All went well; almost suspiciously well. Turning for home, I was poised exactly where I wanted to be, just behind Tie Anchor in second place. I chose my moment to take up the running, approaching the final flight, and I have to confess I was then virtually counting my chickens. Nothing, I thought, could catch us now; I was about to ride my first Festival winner.

What happened next is still a little painful to recall, although I must have relived it a hundred times since. Broadsword, with the race at his mercy, simply tied up on the long uphill run-in. There was no more I could do other than sit and suffer, giving him all the help I could. I sensed rather than saw or heard another horse ranging up alongside to take the prize from us at the last gasp, and it seems oddly ironical now that the winner was to be Baron Blakeney. For if Broadsword was responsible for establishing my name as a jockey, Baron Blakeney did as much to bring the name of trainer Martin Pipe into the racing public's consciousness. Martin's yard has never stopped developing and achieving in succeeding years, and I now find myself riding the majority of his runners. Strange world.

Despite that defeat – one of the most depressing days I have had in racing – I remained convinced that Broadsword could be the champion hurdler the following season. My convictions were strengthened by the belief that the top hurdlers that year were a relatively mediocre bunch. I felt that Broadsword had only to make the normal progress one would expect of a three-year-old turning four for us to have every chance. That progress, however, was elusive. In his second season of jumping, Broadsword was repeatedly and puzzlingly beaten, sometimes by horses I considered to be in an inferior class. My confidence diminished but, come March, the bookies made us favourite again. Our tactics remained largely unchanged and the race followed a similar pattern to the Triumph. Once more, I was perfectly happy turning into the straight. Ekbalco, the horse I regarded as our most serious rival, had made his move to the front along with the Irish challenger, For Auction, but I still felt I had petrol in the tank and I challenged them at the last, going for a narrow gap between horses. The gap closed even as I made my move and Broadsword, disappointed to be checked, lost his momentum. He finished third, For Auction winning at 40 to 1. I had still not ridden a Cheltenham winner, while Broadsword had again been deprived of the ultimate recognition.

Undaunted, I continued to have ambitions for the horse. Although an entire, I thought he would make a marvellous chaser, and when we schooled him over fences at home I was still more excited by the prospect. He loved jumping and was outstandingly good at it; but my view is that he had grown tired of hurdling, worn down by constantly taking on the best. There was only so much speed in his engine and occasionally it had been found wanting. Over fences, where precise jumping counts so much more, I believed he would be revitalised. But it was not to be, and I can't pretend I wasn't disappointed by the decision to retire him and send him to stud, economically sensible though it may have been. Broadsword was a delightful racehorse, not perhaps the best hurdler I have ridden but immensely honest. He did a great deal for me, and I suppose we shall always be associated with one another.

ROLYAT: Other than the staff of Toby Balding's yard – at least, those who have been around a few years – only the obsessional followers of jump racing form will even have heard of Rolyat. He was, it must be admitted, never more than a 'gaff' animal, a horse whose racing would never aspire to greater heights than the second-division country tracks. I think none the worse of him for that, however. Rolyat might not have been a world-beater but he will always have a special place in my heart for providing the first win of my career.

I had been riding as an amateur for almost a full season when it happened and, if I am honest, I was beginning to despair of ever getting that elusive winner. I had not been short of chances but somehow that magical combination of the right horse, the right race and the right amount of luck had never quite gelled. Although my heart was devoted to racing, I was going through the motions of arranging another career to fall back on, working for an estate agent near my home in Stow-on-the-Wold. The boss was very good about letting me off work to ride, often at very short notice, and no objections were raised when a call came through asking me to go to Devon to ride Rolyat in an amateur riders' hurdle. It transpired that Toby had watched me ride in a point-to-point some weeks earlier, and when his regular amateur Jim Wilson became unavailable for Rolyat he reached me through the secretary at David Nicholson's yard, where I was riding out in the mornings.

Despite all the winners I have ridden since, many of them at a far higher level, my recall of that day remains crystal clear and smugly pleasurable. I had to ride light, so after leaving the office I went first to Gloucester and sat in a Turkish bath I used regularly at that time. Then, in my old, second-hand car, I motored down to the course on the edge of Haldon Hill, north-west of Exeter.

The horse was fancied, there was no doubt about that, and my instructions from the trainer were to jump off smartly and attempt to make all the running over the three-mile trip. I failed dismally to put the first part of the plan into operation as, to my horror, Rolyat whipped round at the start, even as the tapes were raised, and we were left a few lengths adrift of the field. Thankfully, that proved to be the end of his petulance. He took a strong hold, made up most of the lost ground before jumping the first flight and was in front before the second. There, to a feeling of ecstatic relief that I had often imagined but never previously experienced, he stayed.

A few weeks later, Rolyat was entered for the *Horse and Hound* hurdle, another long-distance race for amateur riders, this time on the very popular Newton Abbot course. I kept the ride, repeated the tactics and, this time without being left at the start, he won again. The 'Horse and Hound' is a fairly valuable and prestigious race for the early part of the season; riding the winner gained me some welcome publicity and some welcome rides. I was on my way. As for Rolyat, he achieved nothing more of particular note. He was never going to be more than a bread-and-butter horse, but he helped me put some jam on the bread and I shall never forget him for that.

BURROUGH HILL LAD: This was an altogether different type of jockey–horse relationship. With Broadsword and, briefly, Rolyat, I was personally involved: I felt they were part of me at certain stages in my career. With Burrough Hill Lad I was simply an admiring bystander, or sometimes an opponent. No one would ever associate me with the horse, yet it is a fact that I was on board for one of his first wins, and for his final win, at Sandown two years ago.

When I first rode this big, almost black horse who was to become such a great steeplechaser, he was handled by Jimmy Harris, who turns out quite a few winners from his base in rural Leicestershire, despite being confined to a wheelchair. It was a spare ride, Jimmy's regular jockey being unavailable for some reason, and it was in a commonplace two-mile hurdle event on the Leicester track. The going was soft and I noticed that most of the runners in the early races were coming away from the rails to the stand side for the run up the straight. Having walked the course before racing, however, I believed I would be better off clinging to the inner; I also decided to kick for home turning into the long home straight, which is not a tactic normally employed on a horse of any class. Burrough Hill Lad won the race all right, but not for the life of me could I have realistically imagined that he would ever be good enough to run at the Cheltenham Festival, much less win a Gold Cup.

At that early stage of his career he gained something of a reputation for sketchy jumping. Soon after my successful ride on him he moved stables, joining the lady who was to take him on to such glory, Jenny Pitman. She did not immediately cure his faults, however. I particularly remember a three-mile hurdle race at Kempton Park; Jenny actually asked me to ride Burrough Hill Lad as she was also running Corbiere, who would be partnered by her stable jockey Ben de Haan. I couldn't accept as I was claimed by David Nicholson to ride a horse called Coromandel; we thought he might win, but the finish was being fought out between the two Pitman horses as they came to the last together. Burrough Hill Lad fell, Corbiere won.

There are some horses – often the big, headstrong types – who suffer over hurdles through having no respect for the small obstacles. They too often try to kick them contemptuously aside, and it takes fences to teach them respect and bring out their jumping ability. I believe Burrough Hill Lad was just such a horse and, although it took a little time for the education to take effect, there was no stopping him once he had learned.

He had made history before I came to ride him again, with the Gold Cup, the King George and the Hennessy among his many major triumphs. Phil Tuck, who had I think been the first jockey ever to ride the horse, took the glory of the Gold Cup win; John Francome rode the horse in many of his other wins. The ride came back to me because Francome had retired and Tuck had been sacked. At the time, there was a lot of opinionated comment about this; there were even those who seemed to think I was morally wrong to take the ride, that it was tantamount to stepping into a dead man's shoes. I could not possibly look at it that way. The merits and justifications of the owner's decision to find another jockey were not my affair; I felt sorry for Phil Tuck, but it was not my position to take any moral stance. I had to look at it as a business offer: I was being asked to ride the best chaser in England, and it never occurred to me to refuse.

The partnership was to be short-lived. He ran in the Gainsborough Chase at Sandown Park, ostensibly en route to another crack at the Gold Cup. This presented a complication, as I had already been asked to ride John Spearing's Run & Skip. I politely excused myself, and John understood. Burrough Hill Lad won the Gainsborough and impressed me enormously, jumping faultlessly and fluently and taking up the running as he liked. I could not see anything to prevent him winning the Gold Cup a second time, but I had reckoned without his suspect legs. A cruel injury, neither the first nor the last he has suffered in his checkered career, ruled him out of Cheltenham. He did not run again the following season either and, as I write, his career is over. My record on one of the finest chasers of modern times is two wins from two rides, and will now stay that way.

CORBIERE: There are inevitably times in a jockey's life when he will profit from the misfortunes of a friend and colleague. Nobody relishes the experience, knowing that it is highly likely that the boot will be on the other foot before too long. Many is the time I have stood in for someone who has been injured; I have picked up a lot of winners that way. But very few substitutions have given me the thrill I experienced in the spring of 1985 when I came in for the ride on Corbiere.

By then, of course, he was already a Grand National hero, having made Jenny Pitman the first female trainer to win the race. Ben de Haan had been the winning jockey at Aintree and Corbiere was always going to be his ride; there are very few who get 'jocked off' a horse having won a National on him. But in mid March, Cheltenham time, Ben suffered the sort of freakish accident that, in a high-risk job like ours, you can well do without. He had piloted one of Jenny's chasers around Wolverhampton, finished in the place-money and walked back to the unsaddling enclosure where, having dismounted, he was soundly kicked by the ungrateful horse, leaving him unable to ride.

27

I had been riding out for Jenny for some while, and on a busy Saturday, with her other jockeys spread around the country and Ben on the sidelines, she came to me for the ride on Corbiere at Chepstow. He was a horse that I had known throughout his racing career and had come to take for granted. I had often ridden against him in novice chases, usually on a horse of David Nicholson's called Ten Pointer, and without ever consciously thinking about it I had assumed that he was a big, robust animal. So it came as a surprise, when I stood against him in the parade ring at Chepstow, to discover that he was nothing of the sort. Corbiere is actually a short-necked, stocky horse who usually carries his head high and will take hold of the bridle only when asked to do so. That, however, is the beginning and the end of his quirks. He is one of the most genuine horses and one of the best, most precise jumpers of fences that I have ever ridden, and what was to follow will remain one of the highlights of my career.

The Rehearsal Chase at Chepstow had cut up into a bad race. Most of the quality long-distance chasers had run at Cheltenham and Corbiere would have been a certainty on his best form.

Everybody told me, however, that he perennially reserved his best for Liverpool and was a different, inferior horse anywhere else. That is very probably true, but on this particular day he did everything I asked. Jenny is someone for whom I enjoy riding, because she is always specific about the needs of each individual horse and will give her riders detailed advice. At Chepstow she told me to kick as soon as we entered the back straight – a good one and a half miles from home – and to make Corbiere's jumping count. I followed the instructions and he won comfortably.

Ben was clearly not going to be ready for the National, and I had made no firm commitments to anybody. This is always a delicate time for a top jockey; the National can provide a good pay-day, but more important than that, for me at least, is to go into the race confident that you have at least some chance of winning. I soon realised that I had a dilemma on my hands. What it amounted to was that I had the choice between the last two winners of the race, Corbiere and Gordon Richards' Hallo Dandy, whose jockey Neale Doughty was also injured.

My instincts were always, I think, to ride Corbiere, and Jenny in her inimitable way, made up my mind beyond doubt. I was sitting in the sauna at my home when she rang up and asked me how much I would want to ride her horse. Before I could summon a suitable answer, she had added: 'I suppose, like most jockeys, you would ride him for nothing, wouldn't you?' She has a persuasive way of putting things! Naturally I agreed, trusting that when it came down to money she would make sure I was adequately looked after.

There are some riding decisions you live to regret – but not this one. Hallo Dandy, partnered eventually by Graham Bradley, fell at the first fence. Of course, I wished neither horse nor rider any harm, but the relief was obvious. They were on the outer, where I would normally have chosen to take up a position. My father had always told me that Nationals were not won by bravado and that, on almost any horse, it made tactical sense to keep to the outside over the first few fences, when the hurly-burly was at its most congested. However, Corbiere is apparently the exception to this rule and Jenny instructed me to race up the inside rail, just as Ben had done when winning the race, and although it was against my instincts, I did not attempt to argue or disobey. I need not have worried. Corbiere knows his way round Aintree better than virtually any horse other than the incomparable Red Rum, and he gave me a marvellous ride, totally without alarms of the kind normally associated with negotiating the National.

He is not a spectacular jumper, but very exact. He likes to get in close to the ditches at Liverpool and I knew enough to trust him to pick up at the right moment. He was foot-perfect at almost every obstacle; I was hardly ever out of the leading group and as we jumped the last fence before the long turn for home, I was in front. John Burke, a man who knows what it is to win this great race, was standing by that fence, having pulled up his mount, Lucky Vane. As I passed, he shouted out to me: 'Go on, Scu, you'll win now.' It hit me then. I thought 'Oh God, I'm going to win the National.' Sadly, it was only a fleeting, heady moment. Going to the second-last, I could hear a horse coming at me. I tried to convince myself that it was one of the legion of loose horses, but it wasn't. It was Phil Tuck, riding for his life on Mr Snugfit. Over the last I still felt we had a chance, as Corbiere was rallying again, but then my good friend Hywel Davies, on that talented character Last Suspect, came with that dramatic late run. We were third, and it was the best ride I have ever had at Aintree.

I have ridden Corbiere several times since and I have a lot of affection for him. I even managed to ride him at Haydock when he scored the last victory of his career. It was a fitting way to end. He was strong and commanding that day, the way I shall always remember him. I have seldom had a better or more rewarding ride.

VERY PROMISING: A horse who always seemed certain to live up to his rather presumptuous name, Very Promising came to the Duke's yard at Condicote in somewhat controversial circumstances. He had been trained by Mercy Rimell to win a number of good hurdle races, including the valuable Panama Final at Chepstow, in which he beat a very highly rated horse of ours called Gambir so easily that he inevitably made a big impression on both David and me.

The following year, 1984, Very Promising ran in the Champion

Hurdle and finished third to Dawn Run. I had been the runner-up, beaten by only a neck on the outsider Cima, and I was still moodily contemplating what might have been and putting it down to my usual wretched luck at the Festival when David called me across to his customary entertainment chalet and told me that Very Promising would now be coming to us. The horse had been sold to Mr John Maunders, who ironically had previously had decent horses with Mrs Rimell, including a very speedy hurdler called Eastern Line on whom I had achieved several wins. I was not likely to ride any more winners for Mrs Rimell in the near future, because relations between her and David were, to put it mildly, strained by the dramatic transfer of her best horse.

David ran him at Liverpool, where he finished second to Dawn Run in a 2 mile 5 furlong race, a very creditable effort. I was already convinced that he would jump fences, but as the following season approached, David was doubtful. He didn't believe the horse was big enough to do himself justice over the larger obstacles. And so another hurdling campaign was planned. But it went wrong from the start, gallingly so in fact, when we were beaten by Mrs Rimell's Gaye Brief at Ascot in what had inevitably been built up, and not without reason, as a grudge match. There were certainly no sunny smiles between the trainers in the winners' enclosure that day.

From there we went to Wincanton; Very Promising was made the odds-on favourite, but he was beaten again, this time by Crimson Embers. We spoke again about switching to novice chasing and, despite his doubts – reinforced by a reluctance to take on Dawn Run again now that she too was running over fences – David agreed at least to school the horse at home. He took to fences quickly and David then began the business of trying to find a suitable race for him, which was surprisingly difficult at that stage of the season. Most of the horses in the yard were very sick with a virus at that time, but Very Promising managed to avoid it and when we took him to Haydock for his chasing début he won quite impressively, considering we had been obliged to test him out on one of the most demanding tracks for a novice to jump round.

I fell off him in his next race at Newbury, just as he was coming to win, but back on the same course for a much hotter event he included Townley Stone among his victims, and David was now convinced that we should go for the Arkle Chase, the two-mile novices championship, at the Festival. I thought he would win but, true to my Festival form at the time and his throughout his career, he was only placed behind the Irish champion, Buck House.

Very Promising's place in my affections was earned in a later win in a very valuable race at Ascot, the H & T Walker Gold Cup. It was the first genuinely top prize that David and I had won together and after so many near misses and disappointments it was a day to be savoured. Since then, of course, I have changed stables and the ride on Very Promising has passed to David's new stable jockey, Richard Dunwoody. More important races have been won, including the 1986 Mackeson Gold Cup, and my view is that he remains a horse who is at his best over the Mackeson distance of two and a half miles. He is by no means slow, but I feel that he does lack that little extra speed needed for two-mile championship events – although anyone who saw the 1987 Champion Chase at Cheltenham might justifiably take issue with me. But, you see, I was on another horse that day . . .

PEARLYMAN: I would be bluffing if I tried to pass it off as just another race, because it was far more than that. It was Cheltenham, it was the Festival and it was the biggest two-mile chase on the calendar, but my gut feeling that this was a very special race did not end there. If Pearlyman was to become the two-mile champion in 1987, he had to beat Very Promising, and that was what was strumming at my nerves as I went out for the race on that crisp, bright Wednesday in March.

There was no legacy of ill-feeling between David Nicholson and me; any difficulties caused by my departure from the yard to ride full time for Fred Winter were by then a thing of the distant past. It was just that I did not think I could bear to be beaten by the horse on whom I had won some memorable races. This feeling, I am convinced, made me a harder rider to beat.

Pearlyman eventually won after an unforgettable battle up the hill with Very Promising. It was, I think, a classic jump race which will remain in the minds of those who saw it for years to come.

Without wishing to sound smug after the event, I none the less have no doubt that Pearlyman would have won comfortably but for making two monumental mistakes coming down the hill. They set him back a long way and meant that I had to go for everything at the last, making it the epic it turned out to be.

At Aintree a couple of weeks later he was, if anything, going even better when we parted company. I have little doubt that but for my fall he would have won that race, too – in fact, I am convinced that he is one of the finest two-mile chasers we have seen for some years now, and there have been some good ones with which to compare him. He is a quite brilliant horse, not inconvenienced by weight or going conditions, and although he has been accused of patchy jumping I have long considered this a mild quirk that he will grow out of.

The paradoxes of Pearlyman are that he was not bred to be particularly quick and that he was no more than a moderate hurdler, his activities being confined to the mid-week midland tracks such as Wolverhampton and Ludlow where his trainer John Edwards (who took him over from his part-owner Willie Jenks) likes to look for easy pickings. To be honest, I had never taken much notice of the horse until, when sent over fences, he suddenly began to appear at the major park courses, not simply to satisfy anyone's ego but because he was expected to win. Win he did, too, on a number of occasions before John chose the Grand Annual Chase, a handicap, as his Festival objective. Although still a novice, he carried top weight of 11 stone 5lb, so when John phoned and asked me to ride him, I didn't show a great deal of enthusiasm. The fact is that I had agreed to ride The County Stone, a decent horse of John Thorne's who I thought might very well win. The County Stone was duly sent off as favourite, but he simply couldn't cope with Pearlyman, who won very impressively under Graham Bradley. There is never any point in self-recrimination when you have made the wrong decision – it happens to everyone in the game at some stage – so I simply made a mental note never again to turn down a ride on this horse.

I didn't really hold out much hope of being asked again. John had taken on Paul Barton as stable jockey, and Paul was in the saddle when Pearlyman slaughtered a good field of handicappers

The Aintree ride of a lifetime . . . Corbiere clears
the last in the 1985 Grand National.

Pearlyman, the best two-mile 'chaser I have
ridden, winning again at his beloved Cheltenham.

**Every British racing fan has heard of Very Promising,
pictured (left) winning Ascot's Embassy Premier Chase . . . very few
have heard of the continental traveller Bas (above), this time
being led out at Hanover.**

Celtic Shot gave me one of my greatest thrills when
winning the 1988 Champion Hurdle for Fred Winter.
Little Polveir (inset) was a game winner of the
Scottish National up at Ayr.

THE DREAM HORSES

**Arkle and (inset) See
You Then, immortals of
different generations –
Arkle the greatest
'chaser of his time, See
You Then three times
the champion hurdler.**

Monksfield and Sea Pigeon battled out some of the most stirring finishes jump racing can produce – this one in the Champion Hurdle of 1979.

at Cheltenham early the following season, again under a big weight. I knew then that the stable was confident he would go on to win the two-mile championship in March, but much was to happen in the meantime. The horse failed twice, falling once and then jumping very stickily next time out. It was around this time that Paul Barton announced his retirement. He had been offered the chance of a restaurant business in Jersey and, although he confided that Pearlyman had almost persuaded him to stay on, he knew it was too good a chance to miss. Once his decision was final, I telephoned John Edwards and told him that, if he wanted me, I would make myself available to ride Pearlyman for the rest of the season, as Mr Winter had no horses who were likely to take him on. John agreed, and my first job was to go down to his yard at Ross-on-Wye and school the horse as he had obviously lost some confidence. He jumped poorly at first, but second time around he was a lot better. It was decided to run him at Newbury, in a race containing most of the opponents he would undoubt- edly face at Cheltenham; he ran away with the race, putting in an absolutely foot-perfect performance and removing any doubts which had existed.

I have seldom been so confident that I would win a Festival race, and have seldom wanted so badly to win.

ARTIFICE: When his stable jockey, Richard Hoare, retired, Somerset trainer John Thorne decided he would ask John Francome and me to ride most of his horses between us. John was at the very peak of his powers at the time and could have had the pick of most trainers' horses if he had asked, so he might have thought it a bit of a cheek to be put down for only a half-share. For me, it was different. I was still on the way up and I saw the offer as a chance to get a decent foothold in the West Country, where there is so much racing at the beginning and end of the jumping season. I decided to work very hard at the job, going down to John's yard to school the horses whenever I could. I soon came to enjoy it, too, because it sometimes seemed as though John had hand-picked his owners in the way every trainer dreams of doing. Most of them were friends, they were all very sociable and one in particular, Paul Barber, became and remains a good friend of mine. It was Paul who owned Artifice, for some years the pride and joy of the stable.

When the great two-mile chasers of the last decade are recalled, Artifice might possibly just fall short of the premier division. I was never confident that he would win a Champion Chase at Cheltenham while the likes of Badsworth Boy were around; but I was also convinced that he would never be too far away from the place-money. He was a fine jumper and a horse who could gallop flat out for two miles, though usually not much farther. Nevertheless, one of his best performances came in the two-and-a-half mile Mackeson Gold Cup at Cheltenham. I kicked early and it so nearly paid off. We led over the last, and half-way up the hill I still thought we would win, but Fifty Dollars More and Richard Linley just took it from us on the line.

I always thought he was at his best at Sandown, where the string of railway fences in the back straight suited him so well. The faster the fences came, the better he liked it, and on that stretch he would just keep taking off and gaining ground, with no encouragement or interference needed from the jockey. He was such a lovely horse to ride in that sense, and I think I got on well with him because I was always prepared to leave him alone and allow him to run his own race.

It was at Sandown that he beat Rathgorman, that excellent northern two-miler, but I suppose the most memorable victory of his long career came at Aintree on Grand National Day 1983, when he won the two-mile chase which opens the card. Other than the Champion Chase it is the most valuable and prestigious race of its kind in the season, and Artifice won it on merit, beating most of the best of his generation. It was a great performance for a twelve-year-old veteran.

The horse was more a family pet than a racing vehicle. Jackie, John's daughter, rode him sometimes and otherwise led him up for his races. I remember her being in tears that day at Liverpool, and I'm not sure that John wasn't, too. He and his owners always made Liverpool week a great social occasion, and after his death a few years ago, quickly followed by Artifice's retirement, a lot of the fun went out of that very special meeting.

HALF FREE: Early on in the 1987/8 season, two depressing announcements were made: Richard Linley, who had been through more pain and distress in the previous two years than many of us will endure in a lifetime, had been forced by persistent injury to retire from riding; and Half Free, a star of the Fred Winter stable, would not race for at least a year due to injury. The announcements were not intentionally connected in any way, yet there was a strong emotional link. Richard and Half Free were inseparable in the minds of racing folk; he had ridden the horse to two Mackesons and a win at the Festival, plus many other more minor victories besides. As stable jockey to Sheikh Ali Abu Khamsin, Richard had sat on a lot of good horses, Gaye Brief of course paramount amongst them, but I would take a bet that none gave him more consistent pleasure than Half Free.

I feel almost fraudulent including Half Free in this section, as his success is so obviously the property of another jockey, but the fact is that I came in for the ride when Richard was sidelined and he is without question one of the nicest horses I have ridden.

There was a time when everyone in Mr Winter's yard was convinced that Half Free would win the Gold Cup. His racing style lends itself to the race and he adores Cheltenham, so their confidence seemed well justified. On the day, however, he plainly failed to stay the trip. He loomed up to challenge at the foot of the hill, as he always does on this course, but then faded tamely away when the pressure told at the last. He has won over three miles, but at the highest class he is very much better suited by two and a half.

When he reappeared early in the 1986/7 season, Richard was still recovering from leg injuries. I took the ride, and Half Free won at a canter. It might not have been a top-quality race, but he could scarcely have been more impressive. As usual, his next stop was Cheltenham for the Mackeson, but he had picked up a seven-pound penalty for the Wincanton win and, I thought, had a lot to do. In this race, however, you can never discount Half Free, and he put up his usual impeccable performance. It was as good a race as you could ever wish to ride in, and I imagine it was pretty exciting fare for the crowd, too. From three fences out there were only two horses left in it with a chance – Half Free and Very Promising – and from there to the line, either one could have been fancied to win at any given moment. Very Promising took the prize, but I don't think Half Free lost anything in defeat.

Richard was ready to resume soon after that, so I rode the horse only twice more. At Huntingdon he should have won a three-horse 'conditions' race, but for some inexplicable reason he pecked badly after jumping the last, handing the race to Western Sunset. This rather summed up the luck Mr Winter's yard was enduring at the time, and when we came to the Cheltenham Festival I was not confident that anything had changed for the better.

Half Free was inked in for the final event of the three days – the Cathcart Chase, a race for which the conditions might have been framed specifically to suit him. I had not been expecting to take the ride but poor Richard was hurt again, this time dislocating his troublesome shoulder even as he was riding Galas Image to victory in the Arkle Chase. It was cruel for him, but a stroke of fortune for me, especially the way the day had been going. I had ridden another of Mr Winter's good chasers, Ihaven'talight, in the three-mile Ritz Club Chase immediately after an amazing, snow-bound Gold Cup, and I had ridden a very bad race. The guv'nor did not mince his words, and the well-merited rollocking left me in no doubt that I would have to be at my very best on Half Free to redeem myself.

Western Sunset was once again my principal opponent. The card was running so late, after the delay to the Gold Cup, that dusk was falling eerily over the Cotswolds as we set off, my plan being to track Western Sunset all the way round and then allow Half Free his head at the last. Although I followed this to the letter, I have to say my heart was in my mouth as we came to the final flight, because I feared Western Sunset was still going the better. But Half Free, as he so often does, found an extra gear, and in a hundred yards he had sprinted clear to put the race beyond doubt and salvage some of my reputation.

Half Free is a horse who will switch himself off in a race, and needs to be kept up to his work, but at Cheltenham you simply have to trust him to pick up and go when he comes round the final bend and sees that familiar hill in front of him.

BAS: When I asked my father where I might go to find a summer job which would keep me in racing, he advised me to try Norway. It was early on in my career, I was not yet properly established in England and I felt that a spell in an overseas stable would be valuable experience. Father had both ridden and trained horses in Norway and still had enough contacts to point me in the right direction.

A trainer named Dennis Holmberg, based in Oslo, gave me a job that summer. There were a number of British jockeys there, some of them full-time, others just for the odd race-day. Dennis's jockey was Martin Blackshaw, so I didn't expect many rides, but when Martin decided it was time to pack up, my chance came. It was then that I was introduced to Bas, the horse who was to become my passport to success around Europe, doing more to get my name known outside my own country than I had ever imagined possible.

Opportunities for steeplechasers are very limited in Norway. They have their Grand National, which these days usually attracts a small number of British entries, but there are few other prizes of any value, so a trainer lucky enough to handle a good chaser will usually look further afield. Bas, whose best effort in the Norwegian National was the runner-up spot, happily travelled the continent, racing and winning in Sweden, France and Germany as well as in his own country.

As most of the major jump races around Europe are run on a Sunday, I was usually able to get on a plane either on Saturday night or Sunday morning and still be back in England in time to ride again on the Monday. Bas become a terrific money-spinner for me; there was one season when he won seven good chases in Germany, hacking up in the country's traditionally most important chase at Baden-Baden. He carried me round Auteuil, the marvellous jumping course in the heart of Paris; he gave me a breadth of riding experience I could never have gained by staying in England; and he provided a source of introductions to many influential people in the world of jumping.

He was a highly intelligent horse, a quick and clever jumper who knew very well that the economical way to jump European fences was simply to aim to clear the white pole that is a feature of all continental jumps. Many also have an intimidating expanse of brush on top of the pole, but you can get through that, and Bas always judged it brilliantly.

Bas never came to England, which was a pity. Although the

fences are different, he was perfectly capable of adapting and I feel sure he was good enough to have picked up some nice prizes here. But maybe that is just being greedy. I already owe Bas a lot, for establishing me in various countries where I might otherwise never have ridden, and for giving me a very good reason to go back regularly to Norway, a country I have come to love.

MRS MUCK: Riding a horse for a friend might sound an ideally chummy arrangement, but I have found that it can be one of the most difficult parts of the job. You so much want to do well, for the friend more than for yourself, that you go out to ride weighed down with worries. This syndrome has affected me on a number of occasions, but never more so than when riding Mrs Muck for Nigel Twiston-Davies.

I have known Nigel since we were both ten years old and in Pony Club together. He lived in the same Herefordshire village as my grandparents, and after going into racing with a variety of trainers (the Rimells, Richard Head and Kim Bailey) it was pure coincidence that he bought a farm in the Cotswolds, I moved next door and we ended up as neighbours again.

Nigel rode as an amateur and had a few wins with Emperor's Gift, a mare owned by his parents. They bred Mrs Muck from her and I think it is no exaggeration to say that she quickly became one of the most popular horses in training. I must also add that I would never have believed it. I told Nigel from the start that no horse could ever win a race with a name as ridiculous as that!

Mrs Muck started out by winning a modest bumper (National Hunt flat race) at Hereford, ridden by Nigel's ex-wife Sarah. I was outside my house when the box came past after the race. I waved them down to hear the news and thought they were joking when they told me she had won. The ability was soon to be confirmed, however, as she went on to win another, much more competitive bumper at Cheltenham. I had confidently told Nigel that she had no chance of beating a horse of Jenny Pitman's called Riva Rose but, although it seemed to me that Sarah had taken Mrs Muck on a tortuous journey round the outside, she won easily again.

I suppose I always knew that Nigel would ask me to ride her when she went over hurdles. In a sense I was dreading it. The moment arrived on a dismally wet day at Cheltenham the following season. She had already been beaten in a Sandown bumper, on firm ground, and I had an awful suspicion that I would have to get off after the race and tell Nigel that she was nowhere near as good as he believed her to be. He thought the world of her, of course – he was entitled to, as he had only one other horse in his yard and could hardly have expected any success so early in his tentative training career. I found myself desperately wanting just to bring Mrs Muck back safely; I could not imagine what I would say if she broke down.

The ground was very soft and I took a gamble by racing up the inside rail. She hardly got her feet off the ground at any of the first three hurdles, by which time we were getting detached from the main body of runners. Gloomily resigned to my fate, I decided I would try to let her enjoy a spin round anyway, and pulled her right to the outside. It was as if I had just put a turbo in her engine. Without further prompting, she quickened up dramatically, began to jump well and galloped round the outside of the field going up the hill before galloping downhill as if she had a gale at her back. It was an electrifying experience, and from two or three hurdles out it was merely a question of by how much we would win.

Quite by accident, I had learned her secret. Sarah had not been so naive after all. Mrs Muck just likes some space, to feel she has a chance to run her race. I have never tried to coop her up on the inner again and, of course, she has gone on to win a lot more races, notably a valuable hurdle at Ascot in April 1987 when my wife Maz, who rides her out every morning, proudly led her up.

Mrs Muck is a tough character. She might not be the best horse I have ever ridden but she is brave and consistent and she has given us all a great deal of fun. There are times when riding for friends can be very gratifying.

CELTIC SHOT In March of 1987, Celtic Shot ran in the Supreme Novices Hurdle at the Cheltenham Festival and ignominiously fell at the first flight. Twelve months later, he was back to win the Champion Hurdle – an unusual, if not unique 'double'. For me, it was a very special victory, not only because this is one of a handful of races of which the jump jockey's dreams are made, but also for the circumstances under which he triumphed.

Celtic Shot is trained by Fred Winter who, as the racing world knows, suffered a serious fall at his Lambourn home early in the 1987–88 season. His recovery, prolonged and painstaking, meant that the reins of the yard were handed down, overall charge being taken by his assistant, Charlie Brooks, and more influential roles being played by the head lad, Brian Delaney, by Mr Winter's family and by the workers – the lads and the jockeys. It was a situation demanding a selfless team approach, the success of which is surely measured by the Champion Hurdle win. If I was pleased for myself, in those euphoric moments after the race, I was lost in delight and admiration for the other 'team members' who had made it all possible.

I include in this number the horse's owner, Mr Horton. He has owned racehorses for a very long time and it is fair to say we traded on his knowledge and experience, not to mention his unshakeable confidence, as the big day approached. He never once lost faith in his horse, even at times when Charlie and I might have been expressing serious reservations.

Celtic Shot had come into the yard the previous season and, despite a modest record in his first term of racing, he gave every indication of ability. He won first time up, with Jimmy Duggan riding; for that reason, the guv'nor decided that Jimmy should keep the ride at Cheltenham. Jimmy might have wished other-wise as he lay on the muddy turf watching the rest of the 20 runners gallop away from him. The ride then passed to me and I managed no better, the horse falling at Wincanton on his next outing. We were then reduced to taking him to Uttoxeter, not a place where Champion Hurdle prospects are commonly found, in order to try and restore his confidence. He finished second and, judging by what followed, the aim was achieved.

It was obvious, when he came back into the yard after his summer break, that he had done tremendously well at grass. He was also noticeably more mature; he schooled impeccably and gave me the sort of feel that only a genuine racehorse can impart. He won his first race at Sandown very impressively, despite a bad mistake at the last, and went on to win a valuable handicap at Cheltenham on Mackeson day.

You dream all your life about riding a horse good enough to

win a Champion Hurdle and yet, when that horse arrives, so too do the doubts. I never even thought of Celtic Shot as a champion until that race at Cheltenham. That day, he was quite brilliant, galloping in a perfectly straight line from the last, dismissing the dreaded hill as if it was not there. Fellow jockey Kevin Mooney told me that evening he thought it was Champion Hurdle form, a comment I was never to forget.

Riding him to such an exhilirating win was great compensation to me for missing the ride on the Mackeson winner. I was claimed for the Winter runner and had to get off Beau Ranger, a horse I had ridden spasmodically over the years when he was with the late John Thorne, and later his daughter Jackie. Now, he was with Martin Pipe and he improved astoundingly to take this valuable and prestigious prize.

By then, I was dividing my time between the Winter and Pipe yards, an arrangement which worked remarkably smoothly and was undoubtedly responsible for my retaining the jockeys' championship. I saw at first hand the methods used by Martin to obtain maximum performance from horses who appeared either to have lost their ability or to have possessed very little in the first place. Jealous rivals and baffled punters inevitably spread malicious gossip suggesting something sinister was afoot down in Somerset; I know different. Martin's secret of success is simple – hard work and a rare dedication to detail. He is a marvellous man to work for, his enthusiasm for even the smallest of winners proving infectious, and although I was disappointed to have missed the Mackeson victory, I rejoiced for him. Later in the year I was to team up with Beau Ranger to win big races at Haydock and Cheltenham and to finish third in the Gold Cup. He proved, I feel, that he is the best 2½-mile chaser in training and a great credit to the trainer who gave me around 90 winners last season.

By this stage, the season was panning out happily in front of me. I felt I was riding well, I had plenty of horses to ride and I could look forward to the major races more than ever before. I still found it hard to believe that Celtic Shot could be a champion this season . . . but See You Then was still around then, and in my heart I could not see him being beaten if he got to the race fit. It is history now that his dodgy legs gave out at last.

Celtic Shot's next run was another big-race win, in the Mecca

Handicap Hurdle at Sandown in December. He had been backed for this competitive event as if he was a stone-cold certainty; at the weights, so he was. But, although he eventually won well enough, he did not impress me. He was scratchy in running and, about a mile out, I honestly felt we had no chance. Something was amiss.

He was back to his best on New Years' Day, winning the traditional rich race at Windsor from a good field. Soon after this, I went to Mr Horton's house for Sunday lunch and I was struck again by his conviction that the horse would win at the Festival. I did not discourage him. I suffered from no shortage of faith in the horse's ability, it was simply that I had been there before . . . I knew how tough it could be to win that race.

My doubts seemed well-founded when we returned to Sandown for the final prep-race and finished a well-beaten second. Celtic Chief, the winner, is a lovely horse and I had won on him several times. I could not, however, understand how he had come to beat us by seven lengths. It was a big margin to reverse.

42

The suspension I was given in late February added to the pressure I was feeling. I kept very fit by running and riding out but I was only able to resume race-riding on the Saturday prior to the festival. Fortunately, I had one very hard ride at Chepstow and I was confident it had been enough to put me straight.

On the day, I rode Celtic Shot in the way Mr Horton wanted him ridden. We did, however, have one particularly nasty moment. Coming past the stands, I had got into a very bad position, too far off the pace and with no clear way through. The horse's class got me out of the mess and from then on, all went to plan. Going to the second last, the writing was on the wall. We were in front and for a few heady seconds all my pre-race worries were forgotten. As the last flight loomed, I sensed a rival closing on me. I thought it must be Celtic Chief and that worried me greatly; it turned out to be the Irish horse, Classical Charm. Celtic Shot rallied to my urgings and stayed on marvellously up the hill.

He is undoubtedly a very fine horse, a worthy champion. Of all the horses I have ever ridden, only Pearlyman has given me such a sensation of true class. Perhaps the best is still to come.

3

THE DREAM HORSES

ARKLE: The greatness of Arkle is perhaps best illustrated by the way his name has become part of the English language. The cricketer Derek Randall was nicknamed Arkle for his effervescent running, jumping style in the field. Randall came to prominence more than a decade after Arkle was at his peak, which is some measure of the enduring public affection for perhaps the greatest steeplechaser of them all. To a great deal of racing folk, the majority (but by no means all) Irish, he remains a hero, and it is said that when he was in his pomp, Arkle was the number one topic of conversation in every pub in Ireland. Having heard the stories and soaked up the legend, I can well believe it. My regret about it all is that I was too young at the time to have any clear memory of his individual triumphs.

My interest in Arkle has a personal aspect. Pat Taafe, his partner throughout his career, is my godfather, and as a youngster I really did sit at his knee, drinking in his tales. Pat was, and still is, a great friend of my father's. Often when he came to England to ride he would stay with us, and I have a vivid memory of the morning after Arkle's defeat by Mill House in one of their early, unforgettable head-to-head duels, this time for the Hennessy Gold Cup at Newbury. The papers, and apparently the English punters too, were crowing that Mill House was the new champion. They wanted it to be true, of course, as the battle between the two fine horses also became very much a match between England and Ireland. But Pat would have none of it. He told us that he would have won easily but for a rare mistake by Arkle at the final ditch; what's more, he told the press the same thing.

Pat's views were widely dismissed as an example of Irish blarney; the English racing public was busy acclaiming a new hero and they did not want to hear the excuses of the beaten opposition. But Pat insisted to us, before he left for home, that Arkle would win whenever the two horses met again, and, of course, he was right. At Cheltenham in the Gold Cup, Arkle was perfection itself and the form was comprehensively reversed. I have watched that race again recently on BBC TV's series *100 Great Sporting Moments* and, although it was a good many years ago and I know the outcome by heart, the sight of that wonderful horse still brings a lump to my throat.

I am not the best man to ask for an assessment of Arkle's qualities. To my eager boyhood mind he was simply a giant among horses; I built him up as an invincible and, inevitably, my godfather Pat became an idol too. At a distance of years, and now as a jockey, I can naturally say that I would love to have ridden Arkle, but I know it is something best kept as a fantasy. Pat Taafe was poetry in motion on the horse. Not surprisingly, he had a deep, devoted love affair with Arkle, and their relationship, their understanding, made the partnership work so wonderfully smoothly. Anyone trying to follow Pat on Arkle would have had everything to lose and nothing, by comparison, to gain. They made up one of those rare but memorable entities in racing, a genuine horse-and-jockey team, and to separate them, even in memory, is inconceivable.

GREEKTOWN: In his time as a jockey, my father Michael won the Cheltenham Gold Cup and the Grand National. I mention this because it often comes as a surprise to people. They remember Mike Scudamore winning the National on Oxo, of course, but ask them about his Gold Cup victory and there is a good deal of head-scratching and a lot of blank looks. Very probably, no one will even manage to recall the name of the horse.

This disparity in public awareness between the two biggest jump races on the calendar is still prevalent today. Jockeys often remark on the anomaly by which an unknown rider can achieve worldwide fame by winning the National, a race which carries a certain amount of luck and opportunism as much as courage and stamina, whereas a jockey who has partnered a truly understanding staying chaser through the classic preparation races and then won the Gold Cup at Cheltenham will hardly be better known than if he had just won a handicap at Newton Abbot. Everyone in the game, when asked, gives their ambition as riding, or training, a Gold Cup winner for the rather pompous reason that to take that race is usually accepted as confirmation of being the finest steeplechaser of a particular year; I think quite a few *hearts*, however, would opt for the glamour of the National.

Winning at Aintree on Oxo left an indelible mark on my father. He has had a passion for the race, in fact for the entire Liverpool atmosphere, ever since, and even if he has no runners to saddle at the meeting he always goes up for the three days. His was a memorable National. Tim Brookshaw, his great friend, finished second despite having only one foot in the irons for the last half of the race; my father hit the front a long way from home and I remember him telling me that the trainer, Willie Stevenson, managed to tell him off for this even in the moment of triumph. His enthusiasm for the race has transmitted itself to me, even if his success hasn't. I am not ashamed to say that my greatest ambition in racing is to win the National. I shall continue to work ten months a year in pursuit of the Jockeys' Championship; that is my bread-and-butter business. But I would give a lot for the luck it takes to win at Aintree.

None the less, I grew up feeling very proud that my father had won a Gold Cup. I am not sure that the race at that time had quite the same impact or pulling power as it does now, though; the television coverage, the massive media exposure and the ever-expanding Cheltenham facilities all help to make the modern Festival a mind-boggling spectacle, with the Gold Cup as its central feature. People start talking about the Festival almost from the outset of each season, aiming horses for this race and that, with the acknowledged championships in mind. I might be wrong, but I have a feeling there was not quite as much glitter and razzmatazz in my father's time. The horse on which he won the Gold Cup was called Linwell and was trained by Ivor Herbert, who has since successfully turned to journalism. I know little about the horse, I have to admit. He is not one of those champions whose names are on everyone's lips, and my only impression of him is that he was a small horse, not at all the imposing chasing type.

It is a purely personal preference, but I shall overlook both Oxo and Linwell in this category of dream horses and choose Greektown, a horse my father never tires of discussing. He was in the mould of the great Tingle Creek, a flamboyant jumper who stood off so far from the obstacles that my father came to the conclusion he might be frightened of touching the fences. He also said that when he schooled Greektown, he would have his breakfast first – he knew he might not get it at all otherwise!

Greektown achieved what today would seem quite astonishing. On his first attempt over fences, he won Cheltenham's Cotswold Chase, of which the modern equivalent is the Arkle, the two-mile novice-chasing championship. I can't think of a trainer who would even pitch a horse into the Arkle without any previous experience over fences, but Greektown apparently won it spectacularly well.

He shared an era with that other fine two-miler, Dunkirk, and I think it a bit unfair that Dunkirk is in many quarters revered rather more. I don't know how many times they met, but I do know that Greektown beat him twice. Horses like Greektown can't last, sadly, because somewhere in their brain there is a quirk. Gassy, extravagant two-mile chasers only rarely settle to become as good over longer trips (Desert Orchid is one contemporary example who has managed it) and Greektown was never going to make the graduation. For my father, however, he was nevertheless a great horse.

Horses with temperaments like that of Greektown usually go very well for one particular jockey and hardly at all for anybody else. This is because they take a lot of knowing; confidence needs to be shared. Once that is achieved, you have a very exhilarating ride to look forward to.

PENDIL: Racing, like any other sport, has its prejudices, its natural bias. Jockeys will always contend that the champion horses of their generation are better than those of any previous era. There is not necessarily any evidence for the assertion; it is just a possessive argument blessed by the smug knowledge that it can never be proved one way or the other. I am as guilty of this as anyone, yet I do make exceptions. Pendil is the greatest of these. More than any other horse of days gone by, I would love to have had the chance to ride him. To me, he was the complete steeplechaser – uncomplicated and absolutely genuine. Horses such as this become public property when they are at their best, and in this respect he was nearly in the Arkle class. The British public had been frustrated in their search for an Arkle of their own, and Pendil was the closest they were to get.

His generation was shared with other fine chasers, such as Lanzarote and Bula. It must have been a marvellous time to watch jump racing, with so many stars in the line-ups. I can base most of my judgements only on carefully studied old news film of the major races, on the form books and on photographs taken at the time. Some of the pictures of Bula, standing off at a fence, are spectacularly good. Again, I can use Desert Orchid as a modern comparison in his style, for on the day he won the King George VI Chase at Kempton in 1986, his sheer athleticism and obvious enjoyment of his work gave the perfect retort to those who persist in complaining that jump racing is a cruel sport. If Desert Orchid, and Pendil before him, had thought it was cruel, they would never have run and jumped in the way that they did. It is the honesty and bravery of horses like this that touch my heart and make me think that I am rather a romantic in this tough game – and I'm not sorry for that.

Pendil and Richard Pitman go together every bit as easily as Arkle and Pat Taafe. Richard, I know, put in the hours to build up his understanding with the horse, and it is a tragedy that they were denied the Gold Cup victory that everyone believed they deserved. If nothing else – and I am sure it was no consolation at the time – it proved that the greatest lure of sport is its uncertainty. If the best always won, there would be no point at all in what we are all doing.

SEA PIGEON/
NIGHT NURSE: It is best for me to speak of these two horses together; they are linked in my mind not only because they were both trained by that very clever and successful Yorkshireman Peter Easterby, but because their simultaneous successes coincided with an impressionable time early in my career. They were, however, not remotely similar as racehorses in any other than the prolific winning of good prizes.

Sea Pigeon was the most exciting and most talented hurdler of his time – exciting because, like Dancing Brave during that wonderful season of flat racing he produced, he had to be held up until the very last stages of a race and then urged on for one electrifying burst which, if timed correctly, would see off any opposition.

I have never seen a horse quicken as Sea Pigeon did – not a hurdling horse, anyway. The problem with him, of course, was that it was so difficult to measure the moment at which to let him go. Make the run a few strides too soon, or a few strides too late, and canny old Sea Pigeon could make his jockey look a fool. He needed an artist in the saddle and, more often than not, he got one. Three of the finest jockeys ever to ride, Frank Berry, Jonjo O'Neill and John Francome, all partnered Sea Pigeon, and the sight of first Jonjo and then John getting everything right when it mattered, in the Champion Hurdle at Cheltenham, are among the most vivid memories of my early years in racing.

Sea Pigeon won the Champion Hurdle in 1980 and 1981, and his epic battles with Monksfield, the darling of the Irish, who had won the race in 1978 and 1979, are part of jumping folklore. Night Nurse, however, had already made his mark on the hurdling game with Cheltenham triumphs in the two preceding years, and by the time I was active in the sport he, unlike his stablemate Sea Pigeon, had made the graduation to chasing.

If Sea Pigeon was the speed horse with the quirks, one who needed tender handling and careful persuasion to produce his brilliant best, Night Nurse was the opposite. Of course, he was not a slow horse – as two Champion Hurdles bear witness – but he was essentially a big, dour animal who would wear down the opposition rather than outsprint them over a few crucial yards.

I think of Night Nurse as the perfect example of a typical Easterby horse. He epitomised the tough, good, modest style of horses which Peter seems to like – and I am a great believer in the theory that one can come to associate trainers with a certain type of horse. Night Nurse was the Easterby flagship for some years and was certainly the forerunner of many other similar, if rather less talented and versatile animals at Great Habton. He used to walk around the paddock before a race with his head down, totally relaxed and paying no outward attention to any-thing around him. He was there to do a job and nothing was going to upset him or deflect him. He was around, it seemed, for years on end, but that was his great attraction; staying power, in

It has been an enormous help to
have a former jockey for a father.
Crudwell (above, left) was one
of his most prolific winners
as a rider; now he trains and,
whenever I can, I ride for him.

**Jeff King, one of the finest jockeys never to
be champion.**

Terry Biddlecombe, family friend and an early mentor.

I know Fred Winter
only as a masterly
trainer. His record
and reputation prove
he was also one of
the greatest jockeys
of all time.

**Charter Party winning at the
Cheltenham Festival – my second
winner in a day at the 1986 meeting.**

**Duelling with John Francome at the
Kempton Park Boxing Day meeting in
1984.**

Artists in the saddle – John Francome on Burrough Hill Lad and (inset) Lester Piggott.

fact, is why jumping stars of his kind will always command more public affection than the one-year wonders on the flat.

Night Nurse never won a Gold Cup and eventually lost his speed over fences, but to the end he remained capable of winning some high-class races. He was heavily campaigned, often in the highest league and against such demanding opponents as Silver Buck, yet he was never discouraged and never gave less than his best. I am sure that Peter Easterby would give a great deal to have another like him.

SEE YOU THEN: It is never easy to assess the merits of a horse while he is still racing, but now that we have sadly seen the last of See You Then, he has to be rated in the same league as Sea Pigeon. He had the power to go on and win his fourth Champion Hurdle, maybe more; he may turn out to be one of the all-time greats, despite the injury which ended his career last season. He achieved so much, so young, that there was a temptation to think and hope there was more, and better, to come. But the head, ruling the heart, always said that he could not possibly enjoy the longevity of horses such as Sea Pigeon and Night Nurse. It has, in fact, required a great deal of patience and a lot of work on his suspect legs to shepherd him through even four seasons of hurdling. He was never going to go chasing, that much is certain, and his anxious trainer Nicky Henderson has done remarkably well to get so much out of such suspect legs.

See You Then was well fancied to win the Triumph Hurdle in 1984. He had only just been bought out of Ireland by Nicky, for an Italian-based syndicate, and with Tommy Carmody riding he finished a close second to Northern Game. The following season John Francome rode him, and although he won a number of times, he arrived at Cheltenham as a 16 to 1 outsider for the Champion Hurdle. Frankly, I didn't give him a chance. I remembered him beating the enigmatic Little Bay by a neck at Doncaster and I simply could not equate that with Champion Hurdle form.

To be honest, I don't think John thought he would win either, but as things turned out he was injured in the preceding race and the ride passed to Steve Smith Eccles. Seldom, if ever, can a jockey have picked up such a wonderful spare ride at half an hour's notice. See You Then slaughtered the opposition that day, and if some of us churlishly assumed it had been a bad race, he was to put us all in our place by doing the same thing in 1986 and 1987. By then, of course, John had retired to start training and Steve was stable jockey to Nicky. He will always owe something to that stroke of misfortune which brought him the ride at Cheltenham, but in fairness, Steve has struck up a marvellous understanding with a horse who has won his Champion Hurdles rather in the style of Sea Pigeon, each time being produced only at the final hurdle (Sea Pigeon would have been held up a few hundred yards longer) and then sprinting clear up the hill.

See You Then would have had unlimited potential had he been a hardier sort, but like too many fleetingly great flat horses, we never did see him as often as we would like. In this instance, the motives for the cotton-wool treatment were not the fat stud fees which await colts off the flat, but the simple necessity to race him as lightly as possible in order that he should remain sound for his one big occasion every year.

4
THE JOCKEYS

IT TAKES A LONG TIME for any jockey to establish an identity. The very nature of the job – playing a supporting role to the horses, with features masked as if in caumouflage by helmet and goggles – dictates that riders can seldom aspire to the popular fame achieved by the more visible stars of other spectator sports. Very few, either in flat or jumping spheres, ever become public personalities likely to be recognised without their working clothes by anyone outside the inner circle of racing. Success on the racetrack is not in itself a passport to public recognition, as I know from an incident that happened to me a short time ago. I attended a function in my capacity as current champion jump jockey. I was introduced to a complete stranger who, on hearing my name, said: 'Scudamore? Oh yes, the jockey – I thought you had curly hair.'

51

Following John Francome as champion, you will understand, has its frustrating drawbacks as well as its pleasures. I have come to accept, quite without rancour, that no matter how many times I may win the jockeys' title, or how many major races I may land, that I will not even begin to rate alongside John as a household personality. Some of us are simply not made that way, and no one who does not possess John's rare mix of natural wit and charisma should make the mistake of trying to imitate for effect. If there are two things I have learned to avoid during my years in the claustrophobic companionability of the jockeys' weighing room, one is imitation and the other is jealousy.

It is not necessarily a mistake for an enthusiastic youngster to copy some of the facets of the top jockeys' riding. Often, of course, it is done unconsciously, and I have frequently smiled in recognition as I have watched a newcomer, trying to make his name, give a passable imitation of one of the idiosyncrasies of Francome's or Jonjo O'Neill's riding. Young jockeys will always be mimics. They have their TV heroes and they yearn to be like them, and whether intentionally or not, they will end up giving impressions. If I say that I never consciously modelled myself on anyone, it is not to deny that I had my idols and that a little of their style may have left its mark on me.

At school I was always a great Jonjo O'Neill fan, and it seemed very strange to end up riding with him, at home and overseas, several years later. Schoolboy heroes do tend to become colleagues within the life of a sportsman, but in my case I never quite overcame the wonderment I had always experienced at Jonjo's style and drive. Unless you were looking for him (which I invariably was) you would often not notice Jonjo at all during the course of a race – until the business end, that is. Whereas eyes were always drawn towards Francome by his sublime control and graceful balance, Jonjo would regularly be skulking towards the back of the field, apparently in trouble and unlikely to take any serious part in the finish, yet still appearing magically on the scene at the final flight to come away and win in that unmistakably vigorous fashion. His secret, I think, was the ability to transmit his own confidence to the horse in positions where other, lesser jockeys would have been transmitting only anxiety.

Jonjo was quite exceptionally good at riding a finish, a quality which John could not claim until towards the end of his career. It was for this, the ability to inspire a horse to almost unnatural speed when it most mattered, that I found Jonjo's riding quite irresistible in my early, impressionable years. For the very same reason, but from an earlier era, I was fascinated by Terry Biddlecombe. And, even now, when his personal luck is as low as it is possible to imagine, I retain an unshakable admiration for Lester Piggott.

It doesn't matter that he was a flat jockey; it is not even relevant, though it is interesting, that he rode over hurdles as a boy. What is so striking to me is the Piggott dedication to his profession. He never said very much and he didn't need to, because his riding spoke far more graphically than any words could have done. As a jockey, he was a man of meticulous preparation, endless self-denial and enduringly brilliant race-riding skills. People used to deflate me as a boy by telling me I was too big even to think of being a jockey. My answer was always: 'What about Lester then?' He was my inspiration and, to a degree, he still is, because my abiding ambition has never been to emulate Biddlecombe or Francome but to achieve in jumping the same prolonged domination that Piggott managed on the flat. It is, of course, an immensely tall order, but it does mean there is no possibility of running short on incentives.

As with horses, there is always a danger when discussing and comparing jockeys of becoming irrationally adamant that those of your own era are superior to those of the past. It doubtless happens in other walks of life too, caused by familiarity with the qualities of your own contemporaries and a reluctance to acknowledge that things could ever have been done quite as well in the bad old days. I have always had a handy equalising factor to this ostrich-like syndrome in my father, who rode successfully in a bygone generation but is still closely involved with the game as a trainer. He considers that there are maybe ten good-class jockeys riding now; in his day, he says, there were twenty or twenty-five at one time. There may be an element of the opposite type of blindness in this ('things were always better in the old days'), but I am not inclined to disbelieve him. We have a lot more jump jockeys scrambling for rides nowadays and it is my view that quantity has by no means improved quality.

53

There has, however, been a distinct change in riding fashions since my father's day. I would know that from photographs, and occasional old film, if from no other source. It is a theory of mine, having now ridden in many countries around the world, that jump jockeys of each nation now mirror the fashions of their flat counterparts. For instance, American jockeys of both codes ride with just their toe-ends in their irons; in Australia and New Zealand, both flat and jumping riders stand up in their irons and whirl their whips, windmill style, down the horses' flanks; the French jump riders, too, are noticeably similar to their flat jockeys. In Britain, this trend holds true for the very good reason that so many jumping horses now come from the flat, whereas in the past they were predominantly slower store horses of solid jumping stock. As the type of horse has changed, the obstacles have also been modified. So, too, have the styles of the jockeys.

I started to watch racing in the mid sixties and the first jockey, other than my father, who was to have any great influence over me was Terry Biddlecombe. Terry was a race-rider of classical skills and sense. His style could be compared to that of Piggott, but as characters they were, and still are, poles apart. Lester's idea of an expansive night out would, I am sure, have seemed extremely spartan to Terry, who adhered strictly to cavalier philosophies. Live for today, as in this game you can never be sure about tomorrow – that, I think, would just about sum up his attitude to the business of life and, from all the stories I hear, he was far from alone in his views. Things are rather different these days. Due partly to the advent of the breathalyser, partly to the simple fact that life is run at a more frantic pace, the larger-than-life characters such as Terry are thin on the ground in our game. Steve Smith Eccles often tells us that he is the last of the breed, and I am willing to believe it!

Terry would not have achieved the success he did without an underlying professionalism, however, and only the foolish were taken in by his belligerent determination to treat each day as a party. Under it all, Terry was very dedicated, and to this young admirer he was also no mean teacher. I used to hang on his words, influenced far more by what he said to me than by any individual part of his riding style. Terry has always been very friendly with my father, and as soon as I was old enough I enjoyed riding out with him in the mornings – he on one of father's impending runners and I on a suitably quiet one. In his familiar, gruff way, Terry would pass on no end of tips, though I particularly remember thinking it odd that he should tell me, quite sharply, 'not to ride so bloody short', when his ankles were habitually up by his ears. 'Biddles' and Andy Turnell, who came along a little later, rode shorter than any jump jockey riding today. Francome, with his show-jumping training, restored what most people would consider a sensible length of leg as fashionable, so perhaps it is true after all that we copy the champions of the day, almost as a mark of respect.

Among the jockeys themselves, respect usually stops short of open admiration. In his era, my father had a tremendous amount of respect for two of his rivals in particular – Fred Winter and Bryan Marshall. He would regularly tell me about their strengths, but in public it would never occur to him to praise them too much because no matter that they were friends, they were still the opposition on a racecourse. Years later, engaged in trying to wrest the championship away from John Francome, I experienced the same syndrome. Of course, I admired John's riding as much as anyone – but I was not going to say so and hand over any psychological advantage.

There were others, too, whom my father would point out as being worthy of close watching. One was Stan Mellor, for his toughness and determination. Elegance never came into it with Stan but, just like Piggot on the flat, prettiness was happily sacrificed for the ability to make horses go forward. Few were as good in that respect. Then there were Bob Turnell's two jockeys – Johnny Haine, the great stylist and hurdles specialist, and Jeff King, so strong he seemed capable of picking up horses and dragging them over the line. Father once told me he thought Jeff was the best jockey who ever rode. I never saw enough of him at his peak to argue, but what sits uneasily in my mind is that 'Kingy' never even came close to being champion jockey, nor did he win any of the really top races at Cheltenham or Liverpool. He was, in effect, a star purely through ability, not achievement. To me, it seems wasteful that a man of such obvious, widely acknowledged talent did not put himself out to become champion, seeking out the appropriate rides. Did he not have the ambition? Or was there an inner peace in him which meant that he wasn't hungry enough to chase glory?

Steve Smith Eccles is, perhaps, a modern equivalent. He has a great deal going for him and should surely have been champion before now, but it is not in him to chase rides, just as it wasn't in Jeff, and while I cannot personally understand the attitude, I am well aware that it probably makes them both happier people than I. The King and Eccles personalities can leave their job behind when racing is over for the day; I have always tended to take it home with me. At times I know I am bloody miserable – when things are going wrong, I am a candidate for euthanasia. This part of me has not mellowed with the years and now I have begun to think it never will. The urge to seek out success, the dread of failure, remains as powerful a motivator as it ever was.

I try never to draw envious comparisons with other jockeys. That, I believe, would simply lead to spending life worrying about what others are doing, when what really matters is my own progress. I set targets and standards against my own past record and, trite though it may sound, my greatest incentive is to go on riding until I am satisfied I have achieved the highest possible standard. Each season I am aware of doing things of which I would not previously have been capable. I know I am getting better all the time, yet I have still never quite recaptured the extraordinary flow of winners which came my way in the 1981/2 season. In 1986/7 I won the jockeys' title again, yet rode only two trebles; five years earlier, I had been riding trebles and four-timers almost as a habit. Even in 1987/8, when I recorded my best total of 132 winners, I was aware of having to work harder for success than in 1981/2.

It was, looking back, an astonishing period of my career, probably never to be repeated. I was on the very crest of a wave and I could do absolutely no wrong. It was summed up rather aptly one day when I went to Ludlow to ride a horse for Richard Francis. I went utterly without hope of anything but a riding fee, because this animal had dreadful form figures and Richard had told me frankly that no jockey had yet been able to make him jump. I set off on what I planned to be nothing more fancy than an educational spin, took the horse right round the outside and won at a canter. (That horse went on to win a decent handicap hurdle, much to the amazement of all connections.)

That was typical of the string of successes, as I raced to 120 winners with a month of the season still to run. I had only to stay fit to be certain of taking the championship from Francome. But, of course, I didn't. I broke my arm at Southwell at the end of April and had to sit around in mental agony while John travelled the length and breadth of the country to draw level with me and then, in a remarkable show of sportsmanship I am not sure I could have matched, called it a day with the title shared. I had a lot of time on my hands then, and I did a great deal of constructive thinking.

I realise that the run of success I enjoyed was symptomatic of that special momentum sometimes enjoyed, as a fleeting bless-ing, by young sportsmen who have suddenly forged a path to public attention. I had only to keep working hard at my riding; the winning horses kept turning up. But when the flow was brought to a grinding halt by that injury, which I now appreciate was bound to happen sometime, it took me quite a while to get going again at what I considered an acceptable pace. Francome was riding better than ever and I was obliged to concede that he also knew far more about the job than I did – not just the riding itself, but the peripheral essentials of communication with the right people and the ability to pick the right horse in a race. After a lot of heart-searching, I knew I had to go back to the drawing-board and improve myself in all manner of ways if I were to earn another chance to take the title from John.

I had always been driven by the urge to prove myself while John and Jonjo were still around. In a sense, I had done it in 1981/2; most racing people said that I was the real champion that year, and John was good enough to make the public gesture which stated that opinion louder than anyone. But it was not enough for me, and in the year or so which followed I think I suffered for the first time from an inferiority complex.

Francome, as I have hinted, had never been a hero of mine, only because I was more attracted by riders in the mould of Biddlecombe and O'Neill who could produce a driving finish. John never had that, at least in his early years, and it was only when I came up against him as a formidable opponent that I became fully aware of the range of qualities he possessed. In the technicalities of race-riding – putting horses in the optimum position, putting them right at the obstacles, and producing them for the vital burst at the most beneficial moment – he was unrivalled, and surely as good as there has ever been. It was also pretty galling that he improved the strength of his finish so much – as soon as I came on the scene, or so it seemed to me!

I never felt that it was impossible for me to be champion while John was riding, but this was certainly a minority view. Everyone else in the game seemed to accept that he was champion for as long as he wanted to be. He was the senior statesman of the sport, a man apart, living on an entirely different plane to the rest of us. The man in the street with only a passing interest in racing would not have known me – or any other jump jockey for that matter – but everyone knew John, his face, his voice and his achievements.

In a way, his retirement created extra pressure for me. With John out of the way, I immediately felt I *ought* to be champion, and that if I failed now there would be no excuses left. There was no possible fear of my losing any will to win once his rivalry had ended. I was never going to be satisfied with being champion once, twice or even three times. I wanted to win it as many times as John, and more, not through any unworthy wish to put him down but for my own selfish satisfaction. Different people have different motives for playing sport; I ride because I want to go on winning the title and winning major races. Once that becomes impossible, I think my love of the sport will vanish because, strange though it may sound to some less motivated people, success is my one driving force.

John, I suspect, was never so single-minded. His interests have always been diverse, his active brain ever ready to dream up another enterprise totally outside racing. Perhaps he is a more complete person for this facility, but there is no denying that we are very different as characters. We were friends because we spent so much time together as fellow jockeys; but we had virtually nothing in common other than a talent for riding winners. That is not to say that I found anything to dislike in him. On the contrary, I consider John to be one of the most amusing companions I have ever met, a master at lifting the mood of a weighing room or a party with the telling of a joke or the playing of a prank. I was probably happier in his company than he was in mine, for the simple reason that I looked up to him.

58

The most striking single difference between us is in what we say – or, in my case, what I don't say. John has often accused me of taking life too seriously, of being too solemn and intense, but it never occurred to me that I was enjoying myself less than anyone else; we simply had our own ways of showing it. What John thinks, he usually says, often with wickedly funny embellishments. I am the opposite, anxious not to offend by telling anyone what I think of them. In this, John is a rarity. He is so open with his opinions and criticism that one could not be blamed for thinking that he might be short of friends and supporters by now; that he is not is a result of his being good enough at his job and engaging enough as a person for people to forgive anything that might have been considered an impertinence, taking it in the spirit intended.

I consider myself lucky to have had a jockey for a father, an advantage John never had. Although his parents were totally devoted to his career, they were not racing folk themselves. Quite possibly this has made no difference at all to the barbed Francome wit and the naked opinions, but I drank in the experiences of my father and took notice when he insisted that the way to get on in this game was to conform – to have your hair cut acceptably short, to dress soberly and smartly and to be unfailingly polite to the people who can and will influence your career. You have to be very good indeed to get away with regularly telling owners and trainers that their horses have no prospects (it may frequently be the case, but I have yet to meet the individual who did not prefer at least a pretence of sugar on the unpalatable pill). John, by and large, did get away with it; so, too, superficially at least, did Jeff King, who was reputedly still less inclined to mince his words if he considered a particular horse more suited to a milk round than a handicap chase. I have to wonder, however, whether either of them did in fact lose rides through their frankness or, more significantly in the long term, whether they sacrificed potential patrons once they had grad-uated from riding to training. John's training career certainly did not take off in the fashion that most of us expected, and although he experienced some unfortunate setbacks with the local council before being forced temporarily to hand in his licence, I wonder if he, too, was disappointed at the response he received after riding so many winners for so many influential people.

I often wondered what John really thought about me when I emerged as a tangible threat to his position. Other than perhaps thinking me a bit dull, though, it is possible that he may not have given me very much thought at all. With his chip shop business, his newspaper columns and his various other outside interests, racing and jockeys did not dominate his mind as they have always dominated mine. John would be good at whatever he turned his hand to – a naturally gifted man.

John and I had different routes into racing: his was via show-jumping, mine through the amateur ranks. I am pleased, at least, that I did not choose simply to join a yard as an apprentice and work my way through the conditional jockeys' system, because I think it is riddled with problems. There are many things, in retrospect, that I would like to have done early in my career. I would like to have ridden more on the flat to sharpen my racing brain; to have ridden more show-jumping in order to deepen my understanding of presenting horses at obstacles; and to have had what I can only describe as more technical training, in order to knock off some of the rough edges of my style. I know, though, that all this would not have been forthcoming to an apprentice. I would simply have been another number on the rota, another youngster battling against a system in which so many are trying to make the grade and so few are going to succeed. In my view, the amateur route – for all the criticism it receives on largely class-conscious grounds – has far more advantages than drawbacks, because one can remain an individual, free to ride in point-to-points, to go hunting and even to ride abroad – a freedom the lad in the yard can never possess.

It is interesting that, of the recent pretenders to the championship, none has come through the conditional jockeys' treadmill. Simon Sherwood, Richard Dunwoody and I all had spells as amateurs, while Mark Dwyer rode on the flat and over jumps in Ireland before coming over to join Jimmy Fitzgerald as retained jockey. This does not mean that no jockeys of comparable ability have been through the jumping 'apprenticeship', but is certainly indicative of how hard it is to establish yourself as being out of the ordinary. A conditional jockey needs a trainer to give him the opportunities to ride winners, as Martin Pipe has done with the very promising Jonathan Lower in recent seasons; only then can ability be judged. But that is just the start of the road to the top. While I was 'flying' in 1981/2, unable to do wrong if I had tried, it seemed a very easy game. Such an illusion cannot possibly last, and my period of subsequent rethinking taught me that to be regarded as a top jockey one must pass the test of time over a decade rather than a season. I still have a bit to do yet.

5

THE COURSES

THERE ARE CURRENTLY 44 courses in Britain staging National Hunt racing. They are as diverse, surely, as any comparable group of sporting venues in the world, ranging from the austere and imposing Ascot to the uniquely homespun Cartmel, from the grandeur and atmosphere of Cheltenham to the rustic, welcoming charm of Sedgefield. Peter Scudamore has ridden at 43 of the courses, his single omission being Edinburgh, which was adapted only recently from an all-flat racing course. Of contemporary jockeys, his experiences and sheer volume of rides around the country put him in a unique position to judge and comment upon the good, the bad and the ugly aspects of Britain's racecourse circuit.

In general, Peter believes that significant strides have been taken during his career to improve standards. With some notable backward exceptions, amenities are better than they have ever been and most tracks, he feels, are anxious to listen to and act upon the views of senior jockeys and trainers on such matters as the siting of fences, stiffness of obstacles and, most important of all, safety considerations. It is this final area which Scudamore believes must still be worked at. He remarks:

'The medical facilities are still sadly lacking on too many courses. The ambulance service is frequently slack and injured jockeys are left for an unforgivable length of time in too many instances. Despite the unstinting work of Dr Michael Allan, the Jockey Club's medical officer, facilities are short and in a perfect world more money should be spent.

'Some people seem to think that sportsmen who sustain injuries, however serious, are worthy of no sympathy – in other words, that they have volunteered for the risk by taking part and that they should therefore get out of trouble themselves. This is crassly unfair and illogical, as the professional sportsman, including the full-time jockey, is earning a living in a vast industry, just like the man behind a lathe in a factory. The very fact that thousands of people pay to watch the sportsman and, in the case of racing, thousands more bet on his ability, surely makes it still more essential that he receive proper treatment.'

This complaint is a generalisation, not aimed at any particular course, and is augmented by a strongly-held opinion that every race meeting should now be equipped with a modern paramedical unit to deal with injuries. But safety matters aside, Peter does have definite views on each of the courses he has ridden round, and he discusses them individually below.

ASCOT: Frankly, I used to detest the place. As a steeplechase course I felt it had grave shortcomings and as a venue for National Hunt racing I found it both soulless and unwelcoming. To my young eyes, the bowler hats on the heads of the gatemen seemed to have endowed these gentlemen with an arrogance of the most condescending kind; more than once I considered them unnecessarily rude and obstructive to jockeys and trainers going about their daily business, while the stories from spectators who felt they were intruding on private parties are legion. What it came down to, I think, is that the Ascot authorities attempted to run every meeting as they do their Royal flat meeting in June; with ordinary jumping people that just won't wash, and I am delighted to say that things have improved markedly in many respects. There are still examples of overbearing officiousness, but they are now the exception rather than the rule. Ascot has come down to earth for the winter game and, if it still lacks the jumping atmosphere of other major courses, that is a result of its size and design rather than any personnel problems. As a racecourse it used to suffer from fences that were too stiff and trappy, and I would not have liked to run a good novice chaser there for fear of ruining him. But in this respect, too, skilful modifications have been made. Ascot is still not my favourite course, but I appreciate the advances which have been made.

AYR: It may frequently be unfair, but it is a fact that jockeys often rate individual courses largely on the success, or lack of it, that they have experienced there. I am sure it is much the same in other sports – a footballer who makes a habit of missing penalties at Highbury is not likely to hold trips to Arsenal in high esteem, while a cricketer who regularly scores centuries at Headingley is going to think Yorkshire the best place in the world. I like Ayr because I am lucky there. Considering it is a very long way from home, and not on my regular circuit, I have achieved a good many memorable wins up there, taking the Scottish Champion Hurdle on Royal Vulcan in 1983 and on Rushmoor a year later, and the Scottish National on Little Polveir in 1987. Having done my gloating, however, I think I am in accord with most jockeys in regarding Ayr as a high-class racecourse, a good galloping track on flat land, with fair fences and very adequate facilities. I would not at all mind going there more often if it could just be moved a little farther south!

BANGOR: Not long ago, my schedule took me to Kempton Park on one day and Bangor-on-Dee the next. It was like being on two different planets. At Kempton, the facilities for jockeys are grade one; at Bangor, there is not a grade to describe them. I recall sitting there between races, looking around me in the shack which passes for a weighing room, and wondering whether the leading professionals in any other top sport would tolerate such conditions. The answer is probably not, but then that is what makes jump racing such a unique blend of sport and endurance both on and off the track. You would not want to stand in the shower area at Bangor for long unless you were happy to risk pneumonia, but very few jockeys have any great objections to riding there because Bob Davies, himself a distinguished former champion, has applied his experience to the clerk of the course's job and made it a very fair track. The sight of spectators standing on grass banks rather than on terraces and grandstands, however, is one of the quaintest in racing. There is still no stand of any sort at Bangor; it would probably spoil the atmosphere if there were.

CARLISLE: One often hears it said that jockeys are received far more warmly on the remoter northern courses than in the metropolitan South. At Carlisle, I found this to be a fallacy. The course had received a message asking me to phone home. It might have been urgent; it might even have been an emergency. I had no way of knowing. Between rides, I went to the stewards' room and asked one of the stipendiary stewards if he would mind me making the call on their telephone as there was not one provided for the jockeys. He refused in a rude, unco-operative way which left me in no doubt that not only did he have no idea of my identity (I had already been champion jockey once and was about to be again) but that it meant absolutely nothing to him in any case that I was riding at Carlisle. Fortunately, this type of individual is an isolated breed on any course. Kit Patterson, Carlisle's efficient clerk, soon sorted out the situation, but it left a bad taste and I was in no hurry to return. I did ride a winner there but my impression is that the course was more demanding and undulating than anything we have in the South, especially the long uphill climb to the line. It can also get very soft and is a genuine stamina test.

CARTMEL: Although both courses are situated in Cumbria, I found Carlisle and Cartmel a million miles apart in virtually every other way. I rode at Cartmel during their spring bank holiday meeting in 1987. It was the first time I had been there, and I certainly hope it is not the last. Over the three days' racing the crowds totalled almost 25,000, with 16,000 there on the Monday, a quite phenomenal set of figures for any course, let alone this remote and relatively tiny track in the beautiful heart of the Lake District. It was apparently not at all unusual, either. I received a great reception from everyone in authority, and from the spectators, and found it a marvellous atmosphere throughout the weekend. It reminded me a little of the Stromsholm course which staged the Swedish National, in that the tight little track winds through woods, past back gardens and is wholly unconventional in its design. Although the track is only a mile round, there is a half-mile run-in from the final fence, the longest in the country. My one reservation is that the course is so sharp I would not like to be riding with too many runners.

CATTERICK: Being so far north into Yorkshire, this is almost exclusively the domain of northern jockeys; I have been

Friends and rivals: (above) Simon Sherwood wins the 1988 Whitbread Gold Cup on Desert Orchid; (right) a team event with Hywel Davies and Steve Smith Eccles; (below) Richard Dunwoody jumps the last in the 1988 Gold Cup.

THE COURSES

**Plumpton, loved by punters,
loathed by many jockeys.**

**Ascot, much improved in recent
years.**

Cartmel, jump racing at its most
rustic.

The new and the old at Devon &
Exeter.

**The backcloth at Cheltenham – a scene of
which I shall never tire.**

Christmas festivities at Kempton Park.

An unpleasant view of Aintree – my fall from Strands of Gold at Bechers Brook in the 1988 National.

THE CHARACTERS

David 'Scouse' Barker (above left) leading me in on a winner; and a gallops conference between Fred Winter and Brian Delaney.

My valet, nursemaid, and friend, John Buckingham.

**Anatomy of a fall: Playschool
comes to grief in a novice chase at
Kempton Park.**

there only once, many years ago it seems, to ride in an amateur jockeys' hurdle race for novices. I remember travelling up with my father, who trained the horse I was to ride. We sustained ourselves on what seemed an endless journey with the thought that we would have a winner to celebrate on the homeward run; we honestly thought ours would take a great deal of beating. What we did not take into account was that the Yorkshire yard run by Michael Dickinson was giving a first airing to a horse they considered pretty useful, too. His name was Silver Buck. Needless to say, we came home empty-handed.

CHELTENHAM: As befits the premier National Hunt course in the country, and probably in the world, Cheltenham is a true test of rider and horse. It demands concentration, skill and sometimes bravery; the incompetent and the foolhardy will very soon come to grief. This is how it should be – bad horses and bad jockeys should not win races at Cheltenham. I often walk the course as it is not far from my home, and I am always struck by a feeling of pride as I do so. It is invariably in such marvellous condition that I feel it must be the envy of visitors, no matter where in the world they have come from. The executive members at Cheltenham are both efficient and enterprising and a season never passes without a whole series of improvements being made, either to the course itself or to the spectator accommodation. There are, I know, those who moan that it has been over-modernised to the detriment of character, but personally I do not for a moment think that anything has been sacrificed to the cause of progress. To ride there is still the greatest of thrills, and I defy any sporting stage in the country to produce an atmosphere such as that which greets the winning horse and jockey after each race in Festival week. It took me a long time to earn a Festival winner's reception and I had begun to fear it would be forever denied me; all I can say is that it was well worth the wait.

Riding Cheltenham is perhaps the equivalent of riding Epsom to a flat jockey – it is better to know the traps rather than to come there cold. It is easier to ride a race over fences when the obstacles are stiff but fair and there are few hidden complications. At Cheltenham the last fence at the top of the hill is the worst, giving you the feeling of jumping out into nothing; a lot of horses come to grief there. Almost as many fall at the fence at the foot of the hill, by which time you are racing absolutely flat out; you have to meet this one right to win your race. On the hurdles course there are a number of places where the inexperienced or the unwary can be caught out: both starting up the hill and at the bottom of the downward run there are turns where a horse squeezed on the inside will automatically be in trouble. These are observations rather than criticisms. I can find nothing really adverse to report on Cheltenham, and long may it stay that way.

CHEPSTOW: This is one of my lucky courses but my feelings for it extend beyond mere personal success. If any course in the country epitomises what National Hunt racing ought to be, Chepstow does. It has none of the snobbery which still prevails at certain of the major courses, but its quality of racing is uniformly high, staged on an outstandingly good racetrack with long straights to suit real racehorses. It is a course which seems unfortunately prone to accidents, of which last season's eccentric void race when the steeplechase course was wrongly dolled off is just one example, but for all that I believe the management to be enterprising and receptive. The crowd, usually sizeable, is invariably friendly and responsive, making it the sort of track every jockey is happy to visit.

DEVON and EXETER: The racing public has a different perspective from that of the jockeys when it comes to the two Devon courses. Both, in their way, are delightful, but the punters prefer Newton Abbot, while the professionals prefer Devon. Set high up on Haldon Hill, and therefore with its share of gradients to negotiate, Devon is nevertheless a fair and demanding racecourse, with good fences and invariably good ground. The management have worked well to attract a better class of horse and it must say something for the place that trainers such as Fred Winter, David Elsworth and Martin Pipe happily and regularly send young novices down there. The jockeys' facilities have been improved enormously in recent years and, if spectator viewing is still not what it might be, I still believe this to be one of the better-class second-division tracks.

DONCASTER: I do not often go to Doncaster, and I am not sorry. It is unarguably one of my least favourite racing venues, for a variety of reasons. To deflate any accusations of southern bias, I have to say that I am extremely glad this course is not in the South. It probably suffers, as do certain other courses in the area, from a flat-racing bias – so strong in this case that I have taken to wondering why they bother to stage National Hunt racing at all. There is no feel for the winter game at Doncaster, and by the things done and said at the course I can only assume they hold jump racing in very low regard. There is seldom much of a crowd here, the atmosphere is among the worst I have encountered and, although they have a potentially outstanding hurdles course, the steeplechase course is abysmal. The fences were widely thought to be extremely poor, although there have been some recent improvements, and the ground usually rides fast. Altogether, Doncaster is a waste of what could be a high-class jumping stage.

FAKENHAM: I will first concentrate on the positive interpretation of Fakenham's features. It stands in a delightfully rural area of East Anglia and it has a certain rustic charm. It is an unusually tight course, not unfair, particularly suitable for a certain type of horse, and there are trainers who swear by it and come here at every opportunity. The alternative view is rather less flattering. It is remote, ridiculously sharp and has primitive facilities quite inadequate for the 1980s. The remoteness, of course, should not be held against the place; because it is a long journey for me does not negate the fact that it is probably convenient for thousands of people in that part of England who have to travel a long way, Huntingdon apart, to see any National Hunt racing. The sharpness of the track is probably no bad thing, either; if this were a conventional course then, being where it is, it might well be less popular. As it is, trainers patronise it for specialist horses, usually front-running types and those who like to be kidded by the tight turns and gradients of the mile-round track. What are not so easily accepted are the conditions at Fakenham, for both jockeys and spectators; from my point of view, facilities are undoubtedly worse here than anywhere in the country. There is no shower, one toilet, and condensation drips on to the jockeys' sweating foreheads from the weighing-room ceiling. It is worse than Bangor, and changes really need to be made.

FOLKESTONE: There was a time when many jockeys looked forward to Folkestone meetings for one reason in particular – all those who lived north or west of London would make the journey together by train. As road travel is one of the most arduous essentials of our job, the British Rail trip to Folkestone used to be especially welcome. Groups of jockeys would often congregate at Victoria or Charing Cross and the atmosphere on the way down would be convivially expectant, far removed from the isolated and often frustrating car rides. The journey home (depending on how the day had turned out) could also be extremely sociable; the jockeys of my father's era, who tended to travel far more regularly by train, have some hair-raising tales to tell of their rail trips. Since the opening of the M25, however, we all drive to Folkestone. More fool us, you might say, because queues still abound and one inevitably arrives tired and irritable.

68

The course itself has very decent facilities, as do all the southern tracks run under the aegis of the Pratts company, but I have previously been disturbed, on walking round, to find holes that have not been properly filled in and, worse, lumps of metal jutting out from the running rail. I recently spoke about this to one of the course inspectors, who assures me that the situation has been improved if not resolved.

FONTWELL PARK: Deep in the heart of rural Sussex, Fontwell takes a bit of getting used to for me and many others but, once there, everyone enjoys what is undoubtedly an out-standingly picturesque racecourse. It invariably attracts a big crowd, sometimes up to 8000 I'm told, and has a friendly atmosphere even on the wet, muddy days which it sometimes suffers at the mid-winter meetings. Best of all, it is an extremely good hurdles track, a mile-long oval with only two hurdles on each straight. I must say, however, that I am no fan of the chase course. It is a figure of eight, all the fences being on the two straight intersections, and the downhill obstacles, particularly the one at the top of the hill and the one at the foot just prior to the water jump, trap a great many fallers. It is a track for specialists, but a track which also attracts a lot of very bad novices.

HAYDOCK PARK: In calling Haydock the 'Newbury of the North' I am paying it the highest compliment I can muster. This is quite simply the best racecourse I visit in the North, and it provides sport which actually bridges the North–South barrier. All the trainers for whom I ride regularly are very happy to send their best horses north to Haydock, knowing that they will find challenging but very fair racing on an outstandingly good track. It is very well situated for most people in the country, being just off a junction of the M6 and very close to motorway connections for the North-East, and from what I have gleaned, the spectator is treated every bit as well as the jockeys and trainers. From my point of view the facilities could hardly be better, the management is very attentive and ambitious, and the steeplechase course, which in National Hunt terms is the ultimate test, makes horses jump uniformly well despite the fact that the fences are big. It is sad to see the recent trend towards small fields, even walkovers, in Haydock's chases. Could this be a comment on the calibre of horses we have available these days?

HEREFORD: Plenty of brickbats are thrown at Hereford, but not from this quarter. It is natural, I suppose, that I should feel a special affection for the course; I was brought up close by, where my parents still live, and my father is one of the nearest trainers to the course. I love the countryside of Herefordshire – I am doubtless more familiar with it than most – and although I accept that the racecourse may not be the best-equipped or the most atmospheric in the country, I still find it has plenty to commend it, not least the way in which it is run. John Williams is, in my view, one of the very best clerks of the course on the circuit, and those who work with him on the management team are equally efficient and understanding. Hereford can be a pretty bleak place on a raw winter's day (the county cricket ground, set in the centre of the course, can be bleak on a sunny summer's afternoon!), but the locals are enthusiastic supporters, the standard of racing is sometimes surprisingly high and the track is perfectly good. The fences are stiff, which draws some criticism, but I feel that to make them softer would simply invite the field to go faster and cause just as much trouble. There is a rogue fence, the last, just off the turn into the straight, but in a recent effort at alteration the management appears to have effected an improvement.

HEXHAM: Just occasionally on the National Hunt circuit you may come upon a racecourse which quite bewilders you. Hexham is a case in point. Who would have thought of finding a course here, in such vast open country that to most of us it really does seem to be the middle of nowhere? Hexham is actually only about twenty miles from Newcastle; it is close to Hadrian's Wall in the Northumbrian border country, and the course itself is set 800 feet above sea level. If you want a picturesque setting, along with invariably bracing winds, this is the place for you. If, as a jockey, you want civilised conditions, try somewhere else. But Hexham, for all its rustic remoteness, is to many people the very essence of National Hunt, and we would all be the poorer if courses like this were to disappear.

HUNTINGDON: There is usually some competitive racing at Huntingdon and it is a very competently run track, but I personally do not look forward to riding there, especially in novice chases. I don't at all like the way the fences are made here – they are far too black and don't have any gorse in them. Quite simply, horses could be excused for finding them very uninviting. There is another rogue fence there, too – this time it is the second-last which traps so many, again because it is situated at the start of the home straight, just off the bend, so that the horses, travelling flat out if they are involved in a finish, and quite likely tiring, have to jump it off balance. There is very little wrong with the hurdles course, which is fast and flat. Being just off the A1, this is again a very accessible course, so it is far from unpopular with most jockeys and trainers.

KELSO: Another of the Scottish courses, but not one to which southern jockeys are likely to venture very often. It is ages since I went there and it really didn't make a marked impression on me. The people were welcoming though, and the crowd does have a reputation for being both boisterous and knowledgeable. Run by my great friend Sam Morshead, the former jockey, Kelso has a claim to fame in that the stands are more than 150 years old. I would imagine they have seen some parties in their time, too. As at Hexham, experience is an advantage in riding round here.

KEMPTON PARK: Boxing Day at Kempton Park is one of the highlights of every season. It is not simply the running of the valuable King George VI Chase which quickens the pulse, it is the entire spirit and atmosphere of the day. The crowd is always phenomenally large, the racing invariably high-class. On any other race-day, however, Kempton is an altogether more mundane place. Its rather grim facade and overwhelming feeling of suburbia mean, for me, that it can never ooze National Hunt racing in the way that Newbury or Cheltenham can. It is predominantly flat-racing country, attracting a flat-race patronage. The track itself is a little too sharp to rate amongst my favourites but Kempton does now boast the best jockeys' facilities in Britain, bar none. The changing rooms are spacious and spotless, the food and drink outstanding, and they have even laid on a pool table for us to while away the waits between rides.

71

LEICESTER: The average spectator at a Leicester jumping meeting gives the unmistakable impression that he would rather be watching flat racing at Newmarket. Frankly, I don't blame him. The place was not designed for our sport – it is sombre, cheerless and quite often depressing, as the rain sheets down on a December Monday. Most of our meetings here are at the start of the week, and the prospect of a three-mile novice chase around Leicester seldom helps me to digest my Sunday lunch. The facilities have improved, the hurdles track is a splendid test of National Hunt-bred staying types, and there are always ample runners here due to its convenient location. But for all that, Leicester does very little to stir the emotions.

LINGFIELD PARK: John Francome always said that Lingfield was his favourite course, and I can quite understand why. It is not only one of the most attractive places on our circuit, but the facilities are also very good and the track itself is excellent. The ground gets very soft indeed amid the winter rains and there is nothing that can be done about this, but it is a minor drawback among many virtues. Set just south of the M25 in that corner of the country where Surrey, Kent and Sussex border one another, Lingfield is genuinely lovely, as its slogan claims. But amid racing folk, its popularity is due more to the fairness of the course and the fact that the fences are splendidly made – wide, inviting and well sited.

LIVERPOOL: The hurdles course at Aintree is one of the best in England. It is a flat, fast, galloping course, where anyone dropping too far off the pace is likely to be in trouble. It is a good tactical test, too, and things tend to happen quickly, demanding an alert mind. If you lose your position on one of the long turns, the race is generally over before you can recover. The Mildmay chase course has one notorious fence, about four from home on the final bend into the straight. I came to grief myself on Pearlyman at this one during the 1987 meeting (I am sure we would have won) and I have seen plenty of other distinguished two-mile chasers, such as Badsworth Boy and Little Bay, suffer rare falls there.

The National course bears no comparisons. It is unique, a one-off, and must be accepted as such. Those who spend their days bleating about the severity of the fences and campaigning for modifications are missing the entire point of the exercise. As my colleague Richard Rowe once said in exasperation: 'Let's let them have their way, take all the fences down and make it a flat race – it would be a lot easier.' The Grand National is a stern test of horse and man; naturally, not all are up to passing it. No one likes seeing injuries in any walk of life, and any which occur to horses or jockeys are to be regretted, but if the fences were scaled down as some would like, the element of danger would disappear from the event and you might just as well play Trivial Pursuit to decide the winner. The great thing about any sport is its challenge, and in our game, there is none greater or more compelling than the National. Of course, there are jockeys who dislike it – Francome used to consider it a lottery and felt he was not able to excel around Liverpool as he did elsewhere – but to me, if you have the right type of horse it is as easy as riding a poor novice chaser round Ludlow or Leicester. Horses are always invited to concentrate at Liverpool, which is a great help, and believe it or not most of them are visibly enjoying themselves, too.

From the time we jockeys arrive at the course on the Thursday morning (currently, and sadly, there is still only the one meeting there each season) we are counting how many fences we must jump before tackling Bechers. There is no point in pretending it is anything but formidable, and you are mighty thankful to see a good stride as you make the final approach. Once past this one, and with Canal Turn negotiated, you enter the most relaxing part of the race, galloping along beneath the embankment and the gypsy settlements, far away from the stands. Once, a few years back, I was riding a tearaway front-running type of David Nicholson's called Burnt Oak. We had gone a very long way clear of the field and, at the point where you turn back on to the course proper, a strong wind blowing towards the stands quite eerily took all racecourse noise away from us. I was faced by vast open country in absolute silence. I couldn't see the next fence, and for one awful moment I was terrified I had gone the wrong way!

Usually in the National you have plenty of company, but, whether or not you jump round and finish – an achievement in itself – you very seldom know which horse has won until you get back past the stands, and then you find out only by asking. There follows the ritual celebration, the champagne in the weighing room, the endless re-runs of the race given by each and every jockey – and then a sharp and deflating sense of anti-climax. Two restricted races follow, for amateurs and conditionals, which gives us all a chance to wind down with a glass of champagne, but to ride in the final event of the day takes a measure of willpower, and the drive home seems endless. No doubt it all passes in a happy haze if you have won the race, but I have yet to experience that. It remains my greatest ambition, and Grand National Day remains my favourite of the entire season.

LUDLOW: People who live in Sussex swear by Plumpton and Fontwell; those who don't merely swear about them. Similarly, I like Hereford and Ludlow because I happen to live nearby and feel a natural affinity for them, but I can well imagine that I might hate them if I lived in another part of the country. Ludlow is an awkward track with big fences and more than its share of fallers; it is crossed by roads at two points, and at either end of the season the ground can get very firm. It is an unusual course, with not only the weighing room and parade ring in the centre of the track but a golf course too. It does have its attractions, however. Ludlow is a lovely old town, the Shropshire countryside is pleasant and sometimes spectacular, and the stately old grandstand looming over the course is distinctive if not exactly well endowed with facilities. Ludlow is another of those courses you need to know if you are to negotiate them successfully. On the hurdles track, the turn away from the clubhouse is so sharp that it is impossible to gallop round; races are won by sitting tight and allowing the unknowing to be carried wide. Similarly, over fences, the final turn into the straight is followed quickly by the third-last fence, an absolute graveyard if you approach it too fast. Every time it catches me out I hate the place – yet I keep going back with a light heart and a slightly wiser head.

MARKET RASEN: Some steeplechase courses deter all but the best horses by making their fences too big and stiff; a few have the same effect by going to the other extreme, with fences which are really too soft. Market Rasen is one such track and although it continues to draw good-class horses, especially from the crack northern stables of Dickinson, Richards and Fitzgerald, it is my impression that many horses jump sloppily there. I would be hesitant about making too strong a case for toughening up the fences, however; it might produce still more accidents.

NEWBURY: This is my idea of the most impressive track in the country, and is certainly my personal favourite among the major courses. It presents a challenging test of stamina but is a scrupulously fair course where there are seldom any acceptable excuses for defeat. The fences are expertly built and I particularly like the way the ditches are built with banking rather than those intimidating boards in front of them that are favoured by many other courses. Two fences cause problems – the cross fence, farthest from the stands, which is on a downhill gradient, and the final ditch in the straight, where horses are frequently casualties through sheer fatigue. The facilities for jockeys are adequate considering the buildings are all very old; there are good changing rooms, showers and, most important, a sauna. As I mentioned earlier, I strongly believe that this should be a statutory facility on every course, but it remains an exception rather than the rule.

My favourable view of Newbury was only slightly blurred by two controversial and costly incidents there last season. In the first, I was fined £500 for my riding of Arbitrage in a handicap hurdle. I was utterly incensed by the implication that I had not done my best on the horse and seriously considered appealing. I finally decided against it, backing my judgement that the horse's subsequent running would vindicate me. Thankfully I was right. The second incident earned me a more severe punishment, a three-week suspension just before Cheltenham, but here I have no complaints. The stewards were right and I had unquestionably done wrong. All I object to is the inconsistencies which plague the stewardship of our racing, and although there was a time when I felt professional stewards would improve the situation, I am now very doubtful. I suppose jockeys must accept that stewards make mistakes, just as cricketers have to acknowledge the human frailties of umpires.

NEWCASTLE: Set in the delightful Gosforth Park, which seems hardly to belong to the depressed industrial city for which it provides a breath of fresh air, Newcastle racecourse is a tough, demanding track, almost two miles round and frequently subject to extremely soft going. Having said that, I come to a standstill; meetings there are generally at weekends, thus clashing with major programmes in the South, which means I have been to Geordieland very seldom.

NEWTON ABBOT: The word most often associated with Newton Abbot is 'fun'. There is a simple explanation for this: most of the racing here is done during August and September, when the weather is warm, the crowds are big and dominated by holidaymakers, and the racing itself not too demanding. It is an ideal start to the season, and a lot of jockeys take the opportunity to base themselves in Torquay for days at a time during the Devon season. Newton might not be quite such fun in mid-winter, but the atmosphere of escapism and enjoyment catches on again at the springtime end-of-season meetings, some of which stretch over two days. It is a tight little course, barely more than a mile round, and the crowd gets a superb view of every obstacle. Prize money here is exceptionally good – sponsors queue up to support the holiday meetings – and although the facilities are on the rustic side, they are quite acceptable while the weather holds good. I have never ridden on a course, however, where there can be such extremes of ground, from the rock hard in August to bottomless mud in December and crisp frost in January. I have felt more than once that there has been too much frost in the ground to race, but Newton prides itself on very seldom cancelling meetings and so far I cannot say that the stewards have ever been wrong to go ahead.

NOTTINGHAM: I can think of a lot of words jockeys regularly use to describe Nottingham, and in this case 'fun' would not be among them. Like its Midlands counterparts Leicester and Wolverhampton, the Colwick Park track suffers from a soulless atmosphere and generally mundane, Mondayish racing, although this may not be the fault of the management. The whole set-up at Colwick Park tends to depress the eye – the buildings are mostly old and neglected, and the course itself, set on an old gravel pit, is hardly picturesque. The ground is generally good, though, and to be fair there is little wrong with the track. For this reason perhaps their jump meetings usually attract a lot of runners (sometimes, it seems, almost as many horses as spectators).

PERTH: It takes me about seven hours to drive from my home to Perth. That might normally be enough to cloud my judgement and sour my view of a place, but Perth does have rather a lot going for it. Apart from being set in one of the most attractive areas of Scotland (especially if you like shooting, fishing or golf), it is a genuinely good track – a flat, galloping course on which a jockey should have no excuses for failing to ride the race he plans. They stage only autumn and spring meetings here (five two-day meetings) and although I am by no means a regular visitor, I have been there a time or two to ride for my near neighbour John Edwards, who is one of the trainers who makes a habit of sending his horses on the long journey up there. I would doubtless be even keener if I were a golfer, with Gleneagles and St Andrews nearby, but I am perfectly happy to return as a jockey, too.

PLUMPTON: More than once at Plumpton I have come back to the weighing room with such a sense of frustration that I have begun to wonder just how long my career would have lasted if every meeting were run here. In all probability I would have retired years ago. Courses like this are no stage for jockeys to show their skills; all too often you are in a field of bad horses all travelling too fast for their own or anyone else's good, plenty of them ridden by riders who are either foolish, incompetent or – in some especially lethal cases – both. One might say that this is not the fault of Plumpton, simply of the horses which run there and those responsible for putting up the jockeys. But I genuinely loathe riding there over fences. The track is set on the side of a hill; there is nothing apparently wrong with the make-up of the fences but horses fall there far too often and for little evident reason. The worst fences are the first down the hill; indeed, these form one of the major accident black-spots of the country. I seldom get good rides at Plumpton, which might add fuel to my feelings, but I honestly believe it to be one of the most unpleasant riding courses in the South.

SANDOWN PARK: This was always my father's favourite course and he would speak of it in the same loving, romantic tones as those of John Oaksey every time he hosts Channel 4's racing coverage there. It has never quite touched my heart in the same way, because it seems to me to lack the rare and special atmosphere which only courses such as Newbury and Cheltenham can create for jump racing. Purely as a racecourse, however, it is held in justly high regard by virtually everyone in the game. The facilities are very good for jockeys and quite outstanding for spectators (the viewing here must be better than anywhere in the country), and it is usually a delight to ride round.

It does have its idiosyncrasies, however. The string of railway fences on the chase course, towards the end of the back straight, doubtless makes for spectacular sport. It can also be a great thrill to negotiate them on horses like Burrough Hill Lad, Artifice, Beau Ranger and Run & Skip, all of whom I have been lucky enough to partner on the course. On a slightly inferior animal, however, you are mighty relieved to get to the end of them. The hurdles track is very fair, although I do not personally like the long run around the top bend to the first flight in the back straight. The ground down the back is also invariably quicker than it is elsewhere on the track and there is a dangerous tendency to go too fast, leaving little left in the petrol tank for the long uphill climb to the finishing line.

SEDGEFIELD: A little like Plumpton (which attracts train-loads of punters from London), Sedgefield is a course which is far more popular with the spectator than with the jockey. I have been there only a handful of times, including twice for jockeys' matches between the North and the South, but I can well understand why the northern boys look upon it with a certain amount of disfavour. The fences slant from left to right in a very uninviting fashion, there is often no grass at all on the top turns, the last fence is a ditch (unique in Britain) and the run-in on the chase course is an exhausting 500 yards. Having pointed out its pitfalls, however, I can only say good luck to Sedgefield. I have been lucky there, and for a small track it is run in a friendly and enterprising way and draws enormous crowds. To many, this is what National Hunt racing is all about, and who am I to decry that?

SOUTHWELL: It was here that I broke my arm in April 1982, when on the verge of being outright champion jockey. The place still holds bad memories and there have been times, approaching the fateful obstacle, when I have allowed my mind to wander back to that day. It is probably a natural reaction, and it does occasionally happen to every jockey at a fence or hurdle where he has had a particularly nasty mishap (I sometimes wonder whether it frightens horses to go back to the scene of a fall), but it has to be arrested sharply. It brings a lapse of concentration, an unforgivable sin during any race; they can occur through complacency during a particularly good run, or through desperation when everything is going wrong, and when it happens to me I try to be sharp with myself. I tell myself that if I don't concentrate properly, the next fence might be the last I ever jump. That usually does the trick. I once heard Lester Piggott say that concentration was the greatest asset of any top sportsman. At the time I thought he was talking rubbish, but I can see now that he was absolutely right.

My own memories aside, there is little wrong with the track at Southwell, but I can not be quite so generous about the facilities. Time was when I swear the tea and sandwiches were produced in the same pot, so disgusting did they taste, and although there have been great improvements in this respect, the changing rooms are still primitive and the shower area intolerably cold.

STRATFORD: Top trainers run good horses at Stratford, which is a great compliment to a course which would never claim to be in division one. It is probably a still greater compliment to the excellent groundsman, Reg Lomax, who is highly respected by anyone who knows anything about racing. Reg invariably produces good ground when other courses can't cope with the elements. He is also a great character, an all-round marvellous man. Being only ten furlongs round, Stratford is inevitably sharp and tends to suit front-running types. If you don't want to be up with the pace, especially in a full field of hurdlers, it is pointless sticking to the inside rail because you are most unlikely to get a clear run. Over fences, Stratford is very fair and the obstacles extremely well made.

TAUNTON: When I was barely out of my teens, I once heard John Francome complaining about Taunton and proposing that the entire course should be ploughed up. At the time, I was horrified – I considered it sacrilegious to speak of any racecourse in this malicious way – but once I began riding more regularly, I had a lot of sympathy with John's point of view. I grew to hate Taunton, which I considered to be a badly designed course populated by bad horses. In time, though, I came to see that my opinion had been conditioned chiefly by the poor quality of the horses I had to ride. I realised that the jockeys with a supply-line of Taunton winners from the major West Country stables were rather fond of the place, and more recently, with the pick of Martin Pipe's horses to ride, I have come to see why. I would still not put it among my favourite places, but suddenly it doesn't seem nearly so bad!

TOWCESTER: The most contentious feature of the Towcester track as far as I am concerned is its water jump. In fact, water jumps are a matter for heated debate wherever they appear. There are those who decry them as dangerous and utterly dispensable, but being something of a traditionalist, I would not really like to see them disappear. I once fell twice in succession at the Towcester water and I concede that it does cause problems, possibly not eased by the fact that no trainer of my acquaintance ever schools horses over them. They are, however, an intrinsic part of the jumping circuit and I don't see why they should be outlawed. Of all the water-jumps I have encountered, the most awkward was Ayr, and the most fearsome Auteuil, in Paris. At Ayr the sun tended to glint quite distractingly and there was a protruding lip to the landing side which caused a lot of falls; at Auteuil the water is simply enormous – far bigger than anything we have to contend with in Britain. Ayr's water has been done away with, but Auteuil, like Towcester, persists with tradition, just as I think they should.

This apart, I consider Towcester to be a very good racecourse. Despite its undulations, the fences are well made and horses usually jump them very happily. Until recently, the jockeys' amenities were a disgrace – the shower and the WC shared the same area and the stench was putrid – but some efforts have now been made to improve things.

UTTOXETER: This is another course which takes a good deal of 'inside criticism', but in this instance I think it unjustified. To my mind, Uttoxeter is a good, straightforward country track, well supported and competently run. It was, nevertheless, the scene of one of the most bizarre incidents of my time as a jockey. We were heading down the back straight in a long-distance novice chase, not going any great lick, when I noticed three men sitting in the take-off side of a fence, drinking tea and eating sandwiches. They took very little notice as the runners leapt over them, and those of us who survived the first circuit were curious to see if they had been scared away by the experience. But as we came to the same fence on the second circuit, there they were, probably enjoying a second cup of tea and still apparently oblivious of the obvious dangers. If my memory serves me, I think one of them was actually hit the second time around. It was an unbelievably foolish thing to do, no matter how amusing, and I sometimes think certain racecourses are badly at fault in not being more attentive to such blatant breaches of safety regulations.

WARWICK: A very good hurdle track, Warwick has its difficulties as a chase course for two reasons: the fences down the back straight come at you very quickly, disconcerting the novice or deliberate jumper; and, in my view, there are too many runners in the novice chases. The maximum is now seventeen, which may not seem excessive, but I still feel it is two or three too many. Warwick is one of the oldest courses in the country, but the management is very modern in its thinking, laying on peripheral attractions for the racegoers at most meetings and going out of their way to stage the unusual. Their challenge race between Lester Piggott and John Francome a few years back was a fine example of their enterprise; it packed in a tremendous crowd and created interest in racing among people who would not normally have found it even remotely appealing. More courses like this, and more clerks as positive as Edward Gillespie, would give the sport a welcome shot in the arm.

WETHERBY: I remember Wetherby as a very good track, the pride of Yorkshire steeplechasing folk, but something has clearly gone very wrong. Late in 1987, trainers began to boycott the course after strong complaints that the fences had been mistakenly modified so that they were unreasonably severe. This made me cross, as it was the second time in my memory that Wetherby's fences had been the subject of such protests, and I could not see any relevant excuses for the situation. Making fences too stiff is not only potentially dangerous to horse and rider, it causes unnecessary bad feeling which it can take a racecourse a long time to live down. In Wetherby's case this is a particular shame, because in most other respects it sets a high example.

WINCANTON: Wincanton is one of those places which seem utterly inaccessible unless you happen to live there, but this racecourse is certainly worth battling to find. I have nothing at all to say against Wincanton – to me it is the epitome of what a National Hunt track should be: a fair, well-made course, attracting quality racing and big, genuinely enthusiastic crowds. Almost all of Wincanton's racing is staged on Thursdays and it is almost like having an extra Saturday in the week, for the programme invariably includes a high-class, competitive event worth substantial prize money. Small wonder that virtually every jockey I know is a Wincanton fan.

WINDSOR: This is the only true figure-of-eight course on our circuit (Fontwell's chase track is a figure of eight but the hurdles course goes round the outer in an oval). I don't mind the idea at all – there is plenty of room for everyone and it really doesn't matter where you choose to race, because you are never on the inside for long. The facilities here are terrible, with an ancient, under-equipped weighing room, but although jockeys will inevitably moan about this, it comes well down our list of priorities, on which safety factors are undoubtedly at the head. Here, I have no complaints. Hugo Bevan, despite presiding over some of the worst weighing rooms in the country, is a friendly and approachable clerk of the course who is always willing to listen to anyone's problems. I wish there were more like him.

WOLVERHAMPTON: I have ridden my share of winners here, but I simply cannot summon up any enthusiasm for the place. It is invariably cold and cheerless, with a horribly depressing atmosphere – another of those Midland Monday meetings which no one anticipates with any pleasure. As a track it has its supporters, but I personally dislike the downhill fences in the straight, which contribute to a lot of casualties.

WORCESTER: As for Warwick, my criticism is that too many runners are allowed in the novice chases, but this apart, I think Worcester is a high-quality track, certainly ranking among my favourites. It is, of course, one of my most local courses, patronised by many of the trainers who give me rides, and I have been leading jockey there for some time – all of which helps to boost the enjoyment level. Most people will agree, however, that Worcester provides as good a test of a horse as you can find on the country circuits, which is why the novice events, hurdles and chases, are almost always over-subscribed. The ground can get soft here and the weighing room is a Hugo Bevan special, but these are minor drawbacks on a highly regarded course.

6

THE CHARACTERS

THE HEAD LAD: The head lad is the invisible magician behind a successful yard, unseen by the racing public and unappreciated by all except those within the inner circle of his stable. Faceless he may often be, but he is very far from powerless; if a yard begins to produce a stream of winners, you may be sure that the head lad's influence over matters has been great.

I have come into close contact with three such men during my time as a jockey and developed enormous regard for each of them. It is easy, as a brash young man full of the self-importance which can come with a belief that you, the jockey, are responsible for a yard's winners, to belittle the role played by the head lad – to think of him almost as a menial. The jockey who has any awareness, not to mention any brain, will very soon forget this short-sighted view and accept the truth. Everyone in the yard, from the trainer downwards, must respect the head lad. Some among the lads will probably be a shade frightened of him. Certainly no one will want to upset him – if you do, it is tantamount to insulting the trainer's wife (another must to avoid in any yard).

There has to be a high degree of trust between the trainer and his head lad; any breakdown in this, any major differences which cannot be rapidly resolved, will spread rapidly through the stable, affecting everyone. The trainer relies heavily on his head lad for a great many things, including the intimate details of how a horse has eaten, how another has responded to a certain treatment, or how a third has worked at second lot when the trainer has had to leave early to saddle a runner at the races. In the big yards, a great deal of the trainer's time is taken up with entries, declarations and discussions with owners, not to mention the obligation to go racing almost every day. In an operation of this scale, the head lad is essentially the main man; he is responsible for the everyday routine of the yard, and if he should fall down on his job the entire system disintegrates.

The first of this breed I came to know was Lyn Burrows, head lad to David Nicholson. I grew to like him as a friend and it was Lyn who taught me what relatively little I know about the complexities of horses' legs. It was through watching Lyn that it struck me what a strange and solitary job the head lad has, because, for all the preparatory work he may do on each of the horses, he scarcely ever gets to see the end product. The head lad seldom goes racing; his place is back at the stables, holding the fort. I am sure that this would frustrate me, yet most of the head lads I know seem remarkably content with their lot.

Their knowledge about individual horses is boundless, yet the ability to collate such knowledge and make it work to advantage is not something which could be learned at any school or college. It is a gift, and a pretty special one at that, which enables the head lads of my experience to understand horses in a detailed way that I could never hope to achieve. They know the animals they work with as the rest of us know our close friends and family – the difference being that some head lads have sixty or seventy with whom to acquaint themselves!

Brian Delaney has been in just such a position as head lad to Fred Winter, and although nowadays there are only around forty in the yard, Brian's influence is everywhere. I don't suppose I ever quite realised the power or importance of a head lad until last year, when Mr Winter had a fall, spending some weeks in hospital and several months out of commission so far as running the yard was concerned. Charlie Brooks, young, personable and capable, took over, but Brian's back-room brains became ever more important.

He has been with Mr Winter since 1964 and it hardly needs saying that he has handled some legendary equine stars in that time. The mere mention of horses such as Pendil, Lanzarote and Bula makes the hairs on the back of my neck stand up, but to Brian they were just three more horses to deal with, to learn their idiosyncrasies and to act upon them. His long experience, vast knowledge and memories of the stars make him a fascinating man with whom to talk racing, and many's the time I have wished the frantic routine of the day could just stand still so that I could spend an hour or two with him and his many reminiscences.

Brian gets up at 5.30 a.m. every morning. He has been doing so, he tells me, every day since he started work at Mr Winter's, twenty-four years ago. It is not just an essential starting time, it has grown into a habit that he cannot shake, even on rare days off. He is fifty years old now and has been involved with racing all his life; his father Jack rode a lot of winners in Ireland, and all three of his brothers went into the sport. Brian served his racing apprenticeship with Jeremy Tree, the flat trainer from Beckhampton, but he probably learned just as much during two years in the King's Troop of the Royal Horse Artillery. He apparently rode a lead horse in one of the gun teams which gave shows all around the country, but he says the army food, and the anxiety of memorising all the correct riding positions, gave him an ulcer. I must say that in his present job, requiring a great deal of discipline and with a high level of responsibility, Brian does not strike me as a worrier. He is very strict with the lads, however, and although I obviously can't speak from their standpoint I would guess they all have a great regard for him and emerge none the worse for the discipline.

While Mr Winter was away, Brian whipped the whole yard into shape. There were others who made vital contributions, of course, but the fact that everyone wanted to work and pull together in the guv'nor's absence must ultimately have been down to Brian. It was very impressive. Just as important, and equally impressive, is the way the horses look. Even during my first season as stable jockey, when the yard's supply of winners had virtually dried up and we were all pretty anxious about it, Brian kept the horses looking magnificent.

An equally tight ship is run by Dennis Dummett, who is head lad at Martin Pipe's ever-expanding Somerset yard. By the very nature of the place and its geography, however, things are done a little differently from the necessary regimentation of the Lambourn yards. In Lambourn, and all the other major training centres, operations have to be conducted to almost military timing, each yard pulling out at a certain time and using the gallops and the schooling grounds in their turn, or the system would grind to a shambolic standstill. In Martin's remote part of

Somerset such problems don't exist, although the countryside brings its own complications.

In country yards such as Martin's, the lads (among whom there will be a far greater ratio of girls than one would see in the major centres) might frequently have to dismount while riding out, simply to open farm gates. This relaxed approach inevitably permeates through the yard, but if I say the discipline is not as strict as it is in, say, Mr Winter's yard, that is not to decry either their system or their head lad. Martin and Dennis have worked things out to suit their own environments, and the results they have produced in recent seasons speak for themselves.

I have what I believe to be a good relationship with the head lads in my circle, and hope there is mutual respect. I have certainly come to appreciate just what a bearing they have on my own success or failure – and have also come to suspect that, of all the tipsters who abound in every walk of racing, they are the most accurate. If the head lad tells you at breakfast that a horse you are riding that day will win, you are entitled to expect it to come to the last with every chance.

THE STABLE LAD: Every profession has its dregs, its sluggards and its loudmouths, and that of stable lad is no exception. There are, inevitably, some characters in stables who are bone idle, and some who are inveterate trouble-makers. I doubt, however, whether anyone falling into those categories has ever lasted more than a few weeks in a well-run yard. The duties of the stable lad demand dedication, diligence, and not just a love of horses but an ability to get on with other people. Those who don't fit the bill are very rapidly weeded out by the hard-working majority. This, though, is very far from saying that stable lads are a stereotyped breed, because nothing could be further from the truth. In both background and behaviour they are as diverse a bunch as you could wish to meet. Some were born into racing and have literally spent their lives among horses; others came into the game through strange and unexpected routes – although few, I imagine, arrived in a stranger way than did David Barker, more commonly known to all as 'Scouse'.

The first thing to say about Scouse is that he is a one-off. He had never sat on a pony, much less a racehorse, when he applied for a job with David Nicholson. 'Applied' is also a rather fanciful term, because what Scouse actually did was literally turn up on David's doorstep one evening having made the long journey from Liverpool to the Cotswolds. It would have been easy for David to have turned him down flat and sent him away, but to his credit he saw something promising in the lively little Liverpudlian. Quite what it was I don't know, but David gave him a chance and I don't believe he has ever regretted it. Anyone getting the impression that Scouse has been conventionalised, however, should be quickly disabused. He may have mellowed slightly after so many years in the Duke's yard, but only very slightly. He is still one of racing's lovable lunatics, as a few of the printable stories about him may illustrate.

Another of David Barker's various nicknames is 'Stumpy'. This is a general reference to his appearance on a horse. He has, naturally enough, mastered the basics of riding now, but he will never stand accused of being over-stylish. There has nevertheless been a great improvement since his early days, when his lack of expertise got him into any number of scrapes. I have a vivid memory of one particular morning during my time as stable jockey to the Duke. The guv'nor told Scouse and me to canter our horses up a gallop, away from the rest of the string. Half-way up the gallop, a flock of sheep was idly grazing. There was a gap in the middle of them, and as mine was the lead horse I steered through the flock with no great difficulty. It was the instinct of sheep to crowd together when frightened which was Scouse's undoing. The gap had closed as he tried to get his horse through; they cannoned off one sheep on to another, and the impact was altogether too much for Scouse's shaky balance. He was comprehensively unseated, under the feet of the stampeding sheep. The rest of the lads found this hilarious, and to give him his duc, Scouse's sense of humour allowed him to see the funny side too, once he had got over the bruises to both body and pride.

89

These, however, were nothing compared with the bruises he received on another notorious occasion. Scouse, like many other novice stable lads, wanted to enter for the lads' boxing tournament, which has its finals on a grand gala night in London. The attraction for many young lads is not so much the sport but the clothing voucher for about £30 which goes automatically to every entrant, and the free food which is always on offer during the qualifying rounds. Scouse was not greatly bothered about the boxing itself, nor was he at all well qualified for it. Fortunately, the draw favoured him and he received a bye through the first two rounds. This, remarkably, qualified him for the semi-final of his weight range, where he was to meet a particularly good boxer. Undeterred by this prospect, Scouse had been filling in his spare time by tucking into the copious supplies of food, so that as his boxing début approached he was even more ill-equipped than usual to fight.

There are few people in racing who do not both know and like Scouse. His opponent certainly knew him of old and took pity enough to approach him before they went into the ring. 'Look, you're a mate,' he said, 'I don't want to hurt you, so when I hit you, lie down and don't get up again.' This attempted rigging was, I am sure, suggested with the best possible motives, but Scouse's answer revealed that his main anxieties lay in another direction. 'I don't care where you hit me,' he replied, 'so long as you don't touch my guts.' Sadly, however, poor Scouse diverted from the script. When he was punched on the chin, as planned, he certainly went down fast enough, but then foolishly struggled to his feet again, whereupon his puzzled opponent laid him out properly with a blow which disturbed most of the food he had swallowed in the preceding hours.

Whilst I do not wish to make him out as a lad of endless vices, it must be admitted that Scouse does sometimes drink too much. When this occurs, the customary upshot is that he falls over, and this can occasionally have bizarre consequences. One night, I was in bed and asleep when the telephone woke me. It was another of the Duke's stable lads, an Irishman, and he was in a great state of anxiety. Apparently, he and Scouse had been walking back from Stow-in-the-Wold after a night in the pubs. The road to the village of Condicote, where David trains, has a bank alongside, covered in long grass, and it seems that Scouse had been walking along there, with his Irish friend walking on the road. At some stage, the Irish lad noticed that Scouse had disappeared. It was pitch dark and deathly silent, and he panicked. It was not the first time I had been summoned to rescue Scouse at an unlikely hour, and I had an idea of how we would find him. I drove very slowly along the road, my headlights on full beam picking up the grassy bank, while the Irish lad walked alongside. Eventually, the lights located a patch of flattened grass and there, fast asleep, was D. Barker Esquire.

Scouse was the first person in David Nicholson's yard I ever genuinely befriended, and I have since been fascinated by his tactics with anyone new around the place. For a day or two he will deliberately speak louder and more often than usual, simply to get noticed. He will also speak about the newcomer, within his hearing, just to be certain of getting a reaction. The result is that within forty-eight hours he either hates the person or regards him as a lifelong friend.

Although I am no longer attached to that yard, I still see quite a bit of Scouse. He comes to my house to do odd jobs, especially in the summer, and although in many ways we are worlds apart, I think a lot of him. He is the type of character who makes an impression on everyone he meets, and although he may exasperate most of us pretty regularly, he is impossible to dislike.

THE PUNTER: The quickest way for a jockey to arouse official suspicion is to give a professional punter a lift to the races; the tongues will be wagging as soon as they draw into the car park. One punter, however, is generally regarded as an exception to this rule. His name is Simon McCartney, but on the racecourse he is known only as the 'Dodger'. It is a name which suits him well, because a close study of his movements on any race-day would show him doing a fair bit of dodging, either in and out of the crowds to locate the particular trainer whose opinions he wants, or in and out of the betting ring to put the information to good use. The nickname, however, is in this case purely affectionate. The usual stigmas and suspicions attached to punters simply don't apply to Dodger, because everyone in racing knows and likes him as an honest man with a genuine love of the sport.

I have never met anyone quite like Dodger; for sheer dedication to racing, he must be unique. In all weathers, at the most bleak and remote outposts, he will be there, sometimes with his bulky frame covered by outrageously large coats but always instantly recognisable. To my knowledge, he goes racing every day during the National Hunt calendar, and I imagine he is even more agitated than I when the courses fall victim to the virtually inevitable February freeze.

Another way in which he is quite unique is in the reaction he draws from racing people when he approaches them in his brazen manner, which from anyone else in his position would probably be considered impudent at best and downright rude at worst. Very few take offence at Dodger's probing questions because, in many cases, the supply of information is reciprocal.

Dodger gleans a bookful of information on each race, but never puts all his trust in what he is told by jockeys and trainers. He is wise here, as we are notoriously the worst tipsters when it comes to our own horses. Dodger's regular routine involves sitting up half the night with only his form books for company, absorbing everything available about the runners in certain selected races – the races in which he considers there might be a worthwhile bet. Usually, it is only after he has completed his studies that he decides to which of the next day's meetings he will go, and as he lives in Chepstow, this very often involves him in a very early start. Occasionally, I have shared a journey with him and he is without doubt one of the most entertaining passengers anyone could wish to have. He has a bottomless fund of racing stories and a way of telling them which suggests he might have been equally at home on the stage.

Dodger regularly approaches me, urgently waving his race-card, and solemnly advises that I should try to get the ride on a particular horse next time it runs, because it is sure to win. A jockey is always being bombarded with this type of advice, but coming from Dodger it is ignored at one's peril, because he is quite often absolutely right.

Racing, specifically jump racing, is Dodger McCartney's life, and although he is obviously trying to make a decent living from his gambling, there is an infectious enthusiasm about everything he says and does. People trust him because he doesn't buy or sell his information. To the vast majority of people on the racecourse, from the highest official down to the menials, he is a friend. Most of all, he is part of the scene, and if ever a couple of days were to pass without a sighting of Dodger, I feel sure there would be genuine concern for him.

There are times, however, when I reel into the weighing room before racing earnestly wishing I had managed to avoid him. These are the occasions when he has shown you his race-card, marked up with his personal form guide, and against the horse you are due to ride he has scrawled 'NPC' – 'No Possible Chance'.

THE VALET: The first time I met John Buckingham I was a wide-eyed schoolboy goggling at a superstar hero. My father introduced me to him shortly after he had won the 1967 Grand National on Foinavon, following that infamous, extraordinary pile-up of horses at Aintree's relatively modest twenty-third fence. This is a race nobody ever forgets, and John has carried his triumph like a precious label ever since. I had watched the race on TV at home and to me meeting John was every bit as good as meeting the most exotic of film stars. I cannot remember what I said, if indeed I said anything, but I do recall being struck by how very boyish he looked. Normally, to a nine-year-old, even someone in his early twenties will seem pretty ancient, but John had that Peter Pan look about him and, to an extent, he has never lost it.

We are good friends now, but we also have a strict working side to our relationship. When he gave up riding, 'Buck' wanted to stay in racing and the route he chose was as a valet, that hardy breed who pander to the needs of us jockeys, come rain or shine. John looks after a high proportion of the leading southern jockeys, including me, and his duties can be pretty arduous on some of the wetter, muddier racing days of the winter. Apart from putting out the right colours and tack for each of their jockeys at their races, the valets transport their riders' equipment, including breeches, boots and saddle, from meeting to meeting. Quite what would happen if their cars broke down on the way to a meeting I am not sure – thankfully, I have never yet known it happen.

Each of the master valets has a pupil assistant. In John's case, this is Andy Townsend. They work hard, of that there is no doubt, but personally I can see the pleasures of the job, too. All of them are racing types, and valeting gets them involved in the sport and its participants in a way no other job could. They are very much part of the special weighing-room atmosphere, without having the drawback suffered by us jockeys of occasionally having to lie in the mud while twenty sets of hooves pound overhead.

Some of the valets do get involved in the efforts of their jockeys. Andy, for instance, always supports Hywel Davies and is in a much better mood when Hywel has ridden a winner or two. With John, however, neutrality probably results from his own checkered experiences as a jockey; he is just happy to see his charges come back safely, rather than plastered across a stretcher in an ambulance. Because he has ridden, and at a high level, I find John an excellent listener, a kind of father-confessor figure. I tell my troubles to him if things are going wrong and he is invariably sympathetic and very often constructive – he has been through so many similar problems. Like all the valets he has total respect for the sanctity of the weighing room, and nothing that is said there, in anger or in jest, will be repeated outside.

There are times on busy race days when the pressure gets to us all. I can get pretty intense and introverted before a big race, and I am well aware that I must be among the more difficult of the characters John has to look after. Now and again, we will have a tiff, a fall-out, and end up not speaking for a few minutes, often because I think John has given me the wrong weight. I do get worked up about this, it is ultimately my responsibility to weigh out with the proper weight, colours and equipment, but my valet is there to get things right, and I can sometimes be a little short-tempered if I consider he has in any way failed. Fortunately these occasions are rare, and John knows it. Another of the regular southern valets is Tom Buckingham, John's brother, and on days when I become a shade tetchy Tom is a master at cooling the situation by sarcastically reminding me of something I have done wrong in the past. John himself takes absolutely no notice when any of the jockeys gets angry, which makes him such an easy man to deal with, a back-room star of our game.

In truth, of course, there are plenty more like John, men whose quiet, good-humoured efficiency helps the wheels of the sports turn smoothly. Jump racing is lucky. It seems, for reasons I have never entirely been able to fathom, to attract the right sort of people. Breeding, in its popular translation, has little or nothing to do with it; the good guys come from all backgrounds, all walks of life, and end up in the most diverse strands of the racing game. But, with very few exceptions, they blend into the atmosphere of this unique sport and endow it with the magical appeal which, for me, shows no signs of fading. I consider myself very fortunate to be involved, professionally, in a sport where people have retained their sense of perspective, where money-grabbing commercialism is held at bay, and where individuals can still express themselves, and their personalities, without jealousy. It might be a high-risk, high-speed way to make a living; there are those who think we, the jockeys, are quite mad. But I wonder, quite seriously, whether there is a friendlier working atmosphere in such a competitive field anywhere in the world. Long may it last.

PICTURE
ACKNOWLEDGEMENTS
(reading from front of book
pages 1–32)
Gerry Granham: 1 (bottom),
2, 3 (bottom), 8 (top), 9 (top,
bottom), 10, 13, 14, 15, 16,
17 (bottom), 18, 19, 22, 23,
25 (top, bottom), 26 (top,
bottom) 27, (top, bottom
and inset), 28 (top, bottom)
29 (top, bottom), 30 (right),
31
Mark Leech: 32 (5 pictures)
Bernard Parkin: 3 (top), 8
(bottom and inset), 17 (top),
20, 24 (top, bottom), 25
(inset)
Kenneth Bright: 4, 5 (top),
12, 30 (left)
Ed Byrne: 6
Foto-Schafft: 11